instant **EXPERT**

COLLECTING

*G*LASSWARE

MARK PICKVET

Alliance Publishers, Inc.

ISBN 1-887110-05-4

Design by Cynthia Dunne

Alliance books are available at special discounts for bulk
purchases for sales and promotions, premiums, fund
raising, or educational use.
For details, contact:

Alliance Publishers, Inc.
P. O. Box 080377
Brooklyn, New York 11208-0002

Distributed to the trade by National Book Network, Inc.

10 8 6 4 2 1 3 5 7 9

ACKNOWLEDGMENTS

Very special thanks to my wife, Robin Rainwater, for taking photographs as well as allowing me to cover our tables and furniture for weeks at a time with glass-related catalogs, journals, advertisements, books, papers, research, photographs, and so on.

Many thanks to friends and other family members, fellow collectors, antique dealers, auction houses, librarians, museum personnel, glass artisans, university mentors, and glass company personnel: Kate Pickvet, Leota Pickvet, Louis Pickvet, Fairy Pickvet, Juli Pickvet, Robert Darnold, Sue Darnold, Paul Traviglia, Jennifer Hood, Dr. Fred Svoboda, Dr. Arthur Harshman, Dr. David Churchman, Dr. Howard Holter, Dr. Mark Luca, Christine Mack, Barbara Anderson, Richard Blenko, Virginia Womack, M. E. Walter, Susan Boyd, Luke Boyd, Sarah Nichols, Donna Sawyer, Gary Baker, Peter Dubeau, Jane Shadel Spillman, Jill Thomas-Clark, Virginia Wright, Darlene Antonellis-LaCroix, Frank Fenton, Cathleen Latendresse, Jack Wilkie, Lisa Gibson, Jim Hill, Katherine McCracken, Kirk Nelson, Sheila Machlis Alexander, and Sandra Knudsen. Sincere thanks to my agent, Gerry Wallerstein, for constantly working hard on my behalf, and to my editor, Dorothy Harris, for making the book a reality.

Finally, to the glass artisans of the past and present, from the blowers and cutters down to the polishers and packers: thanks for giving us so much.

CONTENTS

INTRODUCTION

What has always fascinated me about glass is the ingredients necessary to create it. Who would ever conceive of mixing sand along with ashes from plants and trees, the two primary ingredients of glass? Furthermore, without knowledge of chemistry and experimentation, who would have thought that certain metallic agents could produce all of those fascinating colors? Indeed, it is gold that gives us the color of rubies; chromium and iron, emeralds; and cobalt, the deepest and richest blue. Lead and even silver provide us with clear sparkling crystal for the purest form of glass.

What do you see in glassware? Is it the color or lack of color? Is it a particular design, era, or pattern? How about form and function? Where else would you place flowers except in a glass vase, or candy in a glass jar? To impress your friends, spread a red-and-white tablecloth for the holidays and fill the table with a complete set of green Depression tableware. Maybe it is the artform itself. Do you like animals or stunning artistic wares? Such items can certainly be found in vast quantities in glass. You've been looking at a particular piece of glass for some time and finally purchase it, or perhaps you receive a glass object as a gift or as an inheritance. You become fascinated and want more!

Such is the way many collections begin. Something within the object itself captures the eye, an emotion, or a need. Once it is acquired, a collector is born. Soon another just like it is found, and then another, and yet another!

Glass collecting is a broad category and covers

everything from Tiffany lamps valued at over $100,000 to souvenir tumblers worth $1. In between are glass items pressed into mechanical machines both old and new, Art Glass products from around the world, brilliantly cut crystal wares, fancy engraved designs, Carnival and other iridescent forms, colored glassware of the Depression era, modern patterns, wildlife items, novelty items, miniatures, and on and on.

The goal of this book is to provide the novice and intermediate collector with a quick but thorough reference guide to glassware. Inside, you will find information on all categories of glassware along with reference information on periodicals, clubs, and museums, and a glossary that includes both definitions and a little information on specific glass companies. Remember that pricing information listed should serve as a general guide to what is happening in the market and is always subject to change.

In conclusion, there is one small favor that I ask of you. If you discover any mistakes, errors, discrepancies, or inconsistencies, or if you have some new or interesting information available that you would like to share, I would be happy to hear from you. Please write to:

Mark Pickvet
P.O. Box 90404
Flint, MI 48509

Please include a self-addressed stamped envelope for a response and adequate return postage for any photographs you might have sent (that is, if you prefer that they be returned). I am away at times but do my best to answer any correspondence that I receive.

I wish you the best in your collecting endeavors.

Mark Pickvet

CHAPTER 1

THE HISTORY OF GLASS

ANCIENT GLASS

Current archaeological estimates of surviving glass objects from ancient Egypt date them to approximately 3,500 years ago. Historians surmise that the discovery of glass may be attributed to a simple accident. Perhaps a wood fire was lit in a sand pit, causing the ashes to fuse with the sand into a glasslike substance. After all, the primary ingredients of glass are silica, a form of sand, and ashes from plants and trees.

Ash is an alkali that helps the sand melt at a lower temperature. Stabilizing substances such as carbonate of soda or lime are crushed into fine powders and added to the batch. They not only assist in the fusion process but also protect against excessive moisture. Metals and other ingredients or additives were varied through the centuries, but the basic formula has, for the most part, remained intact.

The Egyptian technique of core-forming would not change for centuries until the rise of the Roman Empire. The first step in core-forming is the construction of a base or core, ordinarily a mixture of clay and dung. Hot glass was then spun around the core. The core-formed glass was quite dark or opaque and was often decorated with brightly colored glass threads that were woven around it.

The average citizens of ancient Egypt did not usually possess such ornaments as the new glassware. It was reserved for the wealthy, such as high priests, nobles, the pharaoh's assistants, and even the pharaoh himself. Core-formed objects were usually made into containers for ointments, oils, and perfumes. These artistic items have been found buried with mummies in their cases, and even placed in the tombs of pharaohs, next to their thrones.

Core-forming was the exclusive method of early glassmaking, but advances and new ideas followed as the centuries passed. The Mesopotamians cast glass in mold-like containers. Simple clay molds may have lasted for only one good cast, but molds did have their beginning here. Another innovation of the Mesopotamians was the addition of an extra step in the finishing process. After casting, the surface of the glass was polished by revolving wheels fed with abrasives. These basic techniques of mold-casting and polishing would be adopted later by European and American glassmakers.

The second significant step in the history of glassmaking other than its actual discovery was the art of glass blowing. Around 50 B.C., or just over two thousand years ago, the Romans developed the process of blowing short puffs of air through a hollow metal tube or rod into a gather, or molten blob of glass. Glassmakers would heat up a batch of glass to the melting point, inflate a bubble quickly at the end of the rod, and then work it quickly while it was still warm into many shapes and sizes. Glass blowing was the first significant alternative to the ancient methods of casting and core-forming.

With the advent of blowing, glass was no longer a luxury product created exclusively for the wealthy. The Romans produced a great variety of glass, and fortunately a good deal of it survived or was re-created from archaeological digs. The most popular or common items blown were drinking vessels. Drinking cups were primarily used for fermented beverages. Gladiator beakers and souvenir beakers depicting gruesome gladiator scenes, battles, heroes, chariots, and so forth were designed for drinking wine. Glass was also blown into molds, and bottles were often decorated with the same scenery. Other popular shapes blown from glass included figureheads, gods and goddesses, and particularly grapes or grape clusters to celebrate wine and the vine it was derived from. The same grape patterns can be found in nineteenth-century, Carnival, and Depression wares.

The Romans experimented with many styles of decorating that were also adapted later. The Greeks had borrowed cutting techniques from the Mesopotamians but learned to cut shallow grooves and hollows more precisely, in a similar way to cutting gemstones. The Romans advanced further with cutting, engraving, and polishing with the use of stone and wooden wheels. A glass object was held against a wheel and fed with an abrasive paste. Shallow, deep, and fancy cuts were made, depending for the most part on the cutter's skill.

Enameling developed long before glassware. The painting of cave walls, rocks, clay, pottery, and so forth have been a part of every culture since the dawn of civilization. The Romans enameled their glassware much as we do today, but without the complex machinery. With the Romans, colored glass was pulverized into a powder, mixed with oils like a paint, and then applied to a glass article. The piece was then reheated to fuse the enamel permanently. Romans for the most part manipulated cold glass and cold painting. After the fall of the Roman Empire, advances in glassmaking would take place in the Middle East and the Islamic world, and then we move on to Europe for new advances in the history of glassmaking.

Islamic glass dates as far back as the eighth century. The Romans had experimented with some cameo or relief cutting, but the Islamic cutters took it a step further. Relief cutting is a difficult, time-consuming, and expensive process. It involves out-lining a design on a glass surface and then carefully cutting away part of the background in order to leave the original design raised in relief. Relief-cut glass was once again reserved for the upper echelon of society. Plants, geometric patterns, fish, quotations from the Koran, and a wide variety of other designs were highlighted by highly skilled artists in relief upon vases, perfume sprinklers, beakers, bottles, and many other articles.

Common items for ordinary people might include bowls, bottles, and drinking glasses primarily for wine consumption. Enameling was also done on lamps that housed oil for fuel and floating wicks. The period of Islamic glass ended very early in the fifteenth century when, in 1401, the Mongol conqueror Tamerlane destroyed Damascus and captured the glass artisans. He brought them and their skills to Samarkand.

When Europe fell into the Dark Ages, glassmaking nearly became extinct. A few primitive vessels such as bowls and drinking vessels were created, but hardly anything of note for decades. The increase in power of the Catholic Church in the twelfth century was responsible for a new chapter in glassmaking history.

Gothic architecture and the creation of the stained glass window brought glassmaking out of the Dark Ages. Staining materials from oils and vegetable matter were added to the basic ingredients of glass. The development followed of coloring glass with some experimental metals; the glass was cast into flat cakes, cut into small pieces, and then formed into mosaics. Brilliantly colored glass was included in some of the finest European architecture. Huge cathedral windows sparkling in shades of all basic colors adorned the greatest and most elaborate churches such as Notre Dame in Paris and Westminster Abbey in London.

In the new millennium, it is not difficult to understand that the first glassmakers' guild and the hub of the glassmaking world would rise in the city of Venice, which had by the early thirteenth century become the trade center of the Western world. Venetian glassmakers formed a guild to guard their trade secrets as commercial production of glass flourished once again.

The glass industry in Venice was ordered by proclamation to move all operations to the nearby island of Murano. The reason was that the hazards associated with the great furnaces could easily destroy the entire city if an accident occurred in one of the glassmaking houses. The glass trade was such an integral part of the commerce of Venice that Venetian glassmakers were forbidden by law to leave Murano. The penalty for escape was death, though many did manage to escape.

It was not all that unfortunate for the glass craftsmen living and working on Murano. Their skills and reputation were highly regarded, and their daughters were allowed to marry noblemen. For the most part, the city of Venice had a Western-world monopoly of the art of glassmaking. Their craftsmen held the secrets for furnace construction; glass formulas, including the ideal proportion of ingredients, and toolmaking and the use of tools. Knowledge was passed down to their sons or non-relatives, who were only rarely admitted to the guild.

The biggest impact the Venetians were to have on the evolution of glassmaking was the development of cristallo in the sixteenth century. Next to the discovery of glass itself with the Egyptians and the invention of glass blowing with the Romans, the creation of a nearly colorless glass formula was a very significant innovation. The glass was adapted to the world's finest mirrors, far superior to those made of bronze, steel, or polished silver. Venetians produced glass beads for jewelry and rosaries that rivaled gemstones. Glass jewelry was also used for barter in the African slave trade.

Venetian glass was produced in colors that would resurface in Art Glass in the nineteenth century and Depression Glass in America in the early twentieth. Emerald green, dark blue, amethyst, reddish-brown, and later, in the seventeenth century, a milky-white glass—all flowed steadily from the factories on Murano. The monopoly and production of fine Venetian glass dominated the world market through most of the seventeenth century.

Glass was a significant factor in science and technological advances. Clear optical lenses for microscopes, telescopes, and improved eyeglasses and test tubes, beakers, flasks, tubing, and a host of other laboratory apparatus were vital for scientific experimentation. The Venetian cristallo did not react with chemicals, and one could easily observe chemical reactions and the results through the clear glass.

As with most glass up to now, the finest Venetian styles were created for the wealthy. Anyone of importance in the West graced their tables with glass wine goblets, fancy bowls, and vessels created in Venice. The one serious complaint with Venetian glass that surfaced was its inherent frail nature. There was no question that the glass was exquisite and the best made in the world to that point; but it was thin, fragile, and not easily transported; it broke easily in shipment. The quest for a more durable and stronger formula would be taken up by the English.

Shortly after the time of the Venetians, a few other glass houses sprang up around northern Europe. Parts of Europe were still in the midst of the feudal system, and a few glass houses existed near the manors of noblemen. Wood ash or potash was readily available and aided in the melting of the sand mixture. Heavy concentrations of iron in the soil produced glass of a pale or murky green color. These so-called Forest Glasshouses made windows and drinking vessels of poor quality; however, both were very practical items.

In the late sixteenth and seventeenth centuries, Germans and Bohemians began cutting and decorating their glass. Their drinking glasses contained patriotic designs, coats of arms, biblical figures and references, mythological figures, and scenes of daily life. They experimented with the formulas of making glass and actually developed a form of crystal that was easier to cut than the thin Venetian cristallo. In Bohemia and Brandenburg specifically, this new glass could be cut on rapidly rotating stone and copper wheels. The Germans were responsible for the perfection of wheel engraving and engraved many of the same designs as were enameled. As the center of trade in the West shifted away from Venice, so did the advances in glassmaking. The English would adopt the Venetian style and then begin their own unique technological advances beyond the experts at Murano.

This early history certainly has its relevance in the past two centuries of glassmaking. Sand and ash are still the two primary ingredients for the production of glass. Many of the colors used in Art and Depression Glass were invented or even perfected long ago. Enameling, wheel-cutting, cameo engraving, and other decorating techniques can be traced back into the distant past. However, there was still room for significant improvements and experimentation. Both would occur in Europe and America.

England did little in the way of original glassmaking until the seventeenth century. From the thirteenth century, English artisans did manage to produce some window glass and a few crude drinking glasses. In 1571, Giacomo Verzelini and nine other Italian glassmakers escaped to London from Antwerp. Three years later, Verzelini received a patent from Queen Elizabeth to create glass in the Venetian style, using the secrets he was very familiar with. In the next hundred years, England was well on its way to becoming the world leader in the production of practical glassware.

The first significant item that England produced for export was the "black bottle" in the mid-seventeenth century. The color was actually a very dark green, due primarily to iron and other elements present in the sand utilized in the glass formulas. The dark color served to protect the contents from light. The bottle was made of thick, durable glass; unlike the thin, fragile Venetian glassware, the black bottle rarely broke in shipping. Throughout the mid-seventeenth and eighteenth centuries, England was the largest supplier of bottles in the Western world.

A more important goal of English glassmakers was to find a cross between the delicate clear Venetian glass and the strong thick black bottle. They sought the preferred elegance and clarity of cristallo coupled with the durability of the black bottle. The solution arrived in 1676 with George Ravenscroft, an English glassmaker who lived and studied for several years in Venice. He would forever etch his name in the history of glass development by perfecting a formula for heavy lead glass that is still regarded as an excellent formula today.

The new batch held great advantages and was a significant factor in ending the Venetian dominance. When heated, it remained in a workable condition for a longer time, which allowed the glass artisan to indulge in fancier and more time-consuming endeavors. It was superior in clarity, weight, strength, and light-capturing ability. The workability of the first true lead crystal was responsible for a host of new stem formations, particularly in goblets. Air twists, teardrops, knops or knobs, balusters, and others all refracted light as never before. With Ravenscroft's discovery, the English truly succeeded in their goal.

The English further experimented with refraction in their cutting techniques. Prior to the early eighteenth century, England borrowed cutting techniques from the Germans and Bohemians. The new style began with covering the surface of a glass object with an orderly geometric pattern of facets. This technique, combined with the new crystal formula, maximized refraction, which in turn produced a brilliant sparkling effect. This new beautifully patterned cut glass was used for chandeliers, candlesticks, centerpieces, and drinking glasses. Previously, rooms in typical English homes were dark and candles were heavily taxed and therefore expensive. Glass served to lighten the environment and allowed fewer candles to be used—until it, too, became too popular and was also subject to taxation.

Durable glass products from England were exported in large quantities. Some were shipped to the Far East in the seventeenth century, but much more in the eighteenth. The English East India Company exported significant amounts of glass to India, second only to what was shipped to America.

In 1780, Parliament lifted a thirty-five-year ban on the exportation of Irish glass. Irish glass was tax-free, and many of England's skilled glassworkers moved to Ireland. English and Irish glass was virtually identical in style and impossible to distinguish one from the other except for marks. Glassworkers in Ireland turned out huge quantities for American markets across the Atlantic. Glassmaking in cities such as Dublin, Belfast, Cork, and—probably the most famous city for fine glass—Waterford survived well into the nineteenth century. Some, such as Waterford, have been reorganized and continue to operate today.

PRESSED GLASS

America's founding fathers and people who had access to glassware on America's East Coast used British and Irish-made glass well into the 1820s, until the invention of the mechanical pressing machine. Glassware imported by America included water tumblers, decanters, firing glasses, wine-glasses and other stemware, rummers, dram glasses, fluted glasses, finger basins, bottles, punch jugs, liquor or cordial glasses, salts, mustards, butter keelers, globes, and anything else the English and Irish factories turned out.

The American glass industry experienced a shaky start, but it was not for lack of ambition. As early as 1607, the Jamestown Colony settlers included glass blowers. America had an abundance of all the necessary ingredients: excellent sources for ash, plenty of sand, and massive forests for fuel. A small glass house was built the very next year but closed without producing any useful items. The Germans would be the next immigrants to attempt glassmaking in the New World, but with very limited success.

In 1739, a German immigrant named Caspar Wistar built a factory in New Jersey. He hired skilled German glassworkers and became the first commercially successful glass manufacturer in the United States. Just as it had been in the forest glass houses of Europe, the immediate need or practical use for glass products was for bottles and windows. Wistar also made some crude tableware and a few scientific glass vessels for Benjamin Franklin. It was surprising that any glass was made at all, since England banned the manufacturing of glass in the Colonies. The Wistar house, however, did not survive for long.

From 1763 to 1774, another German by the name of Henry W. Stiegel operated a glasshouse in Manheim, Pennsylvania. Stiegel acquired some of the former employees of Wistar's business and hired a few additional experienced foreign workers from both Germany and England. He went bankrupt in 1774, but did manage to create some window and bottle glass. The American Revolution forced his glass house to shut down permanently.

One year after the Revolution, another German immigrant opened a glass factory in America. In 1784, John Frederick Amelung produced a fair amount of hand-cut tableware, much of it engraved. Amelung's factory also made Benjamin Franklin a pair of bifocals. It, too, could not operate consistently at a profit and shut down in 1795.

There were many reasons for these failures even though there was a great demand for glass in the Colonies. Foreign competition and pressure from the British government were significant reasons for those failures. Glass houses or manufacturing plants were well established in England and Ireland, producing large quantities of cheap glass. Early Americans lacked the capital and many of the skills necessary to manufacture glass. Transportation problems resulted in shipping that was too difficult and costly across the Alleghenies. People out West used crude bowls, teacups, and bottles to consume food and spirits.

The Alleghenies were a disadvantage to Eastern manufacturers but a boom to those living in eastern Ohio, northern West Virginia, and western Pennsylvania. The mountains served as a barrier to foreign and Eastern glass long before the great canals were built. In 1797, the first frontier glass house, about sixty miles south of Pittsburgh, was constructed by Albert Gallatin, an immigrant from Switzerland. Later that year, a bottle factory was built in Pittsburgh by James O'Hara and Isaac Craig. This factory was named the Pittsburgh Glass Works, and in 1798, it merged with Gallatin's New Geneva Glass Works. They did manage to produce hand-blown windows, bottles, and some tableware; but they were unable to operate profitably. They sold out to Edward Ensell soon after.

The Pittsburgh and surrounding area was an ideal place to manufacture glassware. Wood for fuel was readily available; later, massive coal deposits were discovered in the region. Large sand or sandstone deposits lie along the numerous riverbeds, and red lead for fine crystal production was available nearby in the Illinois Territory. The commercial markets were wide open in every direction except back East. North to Canada, west toward the Pacific, and south to the major trading centers of New Orleans and the Gulf of Mexico were all available by easy river transport. With all these strategic advantages, early attempts still ended in failure.

America's early successes in glassmaking can be traced to many individuals, but one figure stands out in particular. Deming Jarves not only founded many companies but obtained knowledgeable foreign workers, the proper ingredients, and good formulas, and wrote an important trade volume in 1854 titled *Reminiscences of Glassmaking*. Most important, he was able to obtain enough financial backing to keep his businesses operating long enough to achieve steady profit margins.

In the 1790s, the Boston Crown Glass Company was chartered to produce window glass but managed to do very little. The only noteworthy contribution worth mentioning is that it was the first to introduce lead crystal into America. Many of the workers left and went on to form the Boston Porcelain and Glass Company in 1814. They built a factory in 1815 and made a few limited lead glass products before failing in 1817. Deming Jarves, with three associates (Amos Binney, Daniel Hastings, and Edmund Monroe), purchased the company's holdings and incorporated into a new company in 1818. It was dubbed the New England Glass Company and settled in East Cambridge, Massachusetts.

From the very beginning, the company operated profitably and continuously reinvested in new equipment and recruited skilled workers from Europe. Jarves assumed a leading role as first agent and manager. He was a prosperous businessman and held an early monopoly on red lead production in America. Red lead is a vital ingredient for making fine lead crystal. Jarves left New England Glass in 1826 and went on to form the Boston & Sandwich Glass Company, another successful operation.

What Jarves accomplished in the East, the team of Bakewell, Ensell, and Pears was working in the West. In 1807, Edward Ensell founded a small glass company in Pittsburgh, but it was purchased by Benjamin Bakewell and associates in 1808. Benjamin sent his son Thomas Bakewell and a trusted clerk named Thomas Pears on numerous trips to Europe to hire experienced glassworkers. Thomas Pears split in 1818 to start a bottle factory, but it failed and he rejoined the Bakewells. He quit again in 1825 and moved to Indiana, but came back once again in 1826. He died soon after, but his son John

Palmer Pears became manager of the glass house, and the name was changed to Bakewell, Pears, and Company.

These early successes were somewhat of a rarity. The first period, or what is referred to as the Early Period, of American glass lasted from 1771 to 1830. Several glass companies were founded both east and west of the Alleghenies, but nearly all ended in failure. Cheap European glass and the lack of protective tariffs hurt Eastern glassmakers. Out west, skilled workers were difficult to obtain and the necessary capital was not available to sustain long-term growth and operation. A few economic depressions such as that following the War of 1812 were another factor in those shutdowns. Except for a few enterprising men like Jarves, this first period in American glass history was marked with unprofitability and failure.

The Middle Period was the second period in American glass history and dates from 1830 to about 1880. The Baldwin Bill in 1830 placed import duties and high tariffs on foreign imports. The new tariffs worked, and the glass industry in the United States was given a much needed boost. The American invention of a mechanical pressing machine in the late 1820s led to the mass production of glassware. The invention of this hand press was America's greatest contribution to glassmaking. It was as important as the discovery of lead crystal, glass blowing, and the invention of glass itself. Hand pressing revolutionized the industry; it was very fast, efficient, and could be run with less skilled workers.

Pressed glass was made by forcing melted glass into a shape under pressure. Early on, a plunger was used to force or press molten glass into iron molds. A mold was composed of two or more parts and imparted lines or seams where the mold came apart. With each piece, the mold was reassembled and filled once again. Hand finishing removed some of the marks left by the mold. Molds might contain patterns within them, were usually hinged, and could be full-size single-piece molds or separate for more complicated objects. Candlesticks, vases, common table items, and particularly matched sets of tableware were easily manufactured by hand pressing.

Pressed items were made in great quantities, especially in the factories opened by Jarves. The New England Glass Company, which eventually became Libbey, and the Boston & Sandwich Glass Company were two of the most successful companies producing pressed glass in America. Many followed in the mid-nineteenth century such as Adams & Company; Bakewell, Pears, and Company; Mckee Brothers; Bryce Brothers; Hobbs, Brocunier & Company; and King & Son.

Individual patterns were rarely patented by any one company. Even when patents were obtained, designs were copied. Ashburton or Hex Optic, Bull's-Eye, Cable, Thumbprints, Hamilton, Comet, Grapes, Pineapples, Ribs, Sunbursts, Pillars, Flutes, and so on are at times difficult to distinguish from one company to the next.

One other American invention was the discovery of a cheap lead substitute in 1864 by William Leighton. Leighton, who was employed by Hobbs, Brocunier & Company at the time, developed a glass formula that substituted lime for the much more expensive lead. The glass products manufactured with lime still maintained a good degree of clarity. Though the brilliance was not as sharp as that of lead crystal, the price savings and practicality more than made up for the difference in quality. Most companies were forced to switch to lime in order to remain competitive.

Pressed glass remained somewhat affordable as compared to art and cut glass in the late nineteenth and early twentieth centuries, too. Fire polishing, which was developed in England in 1834, was adopted in America. Fire polishing removed mold and tool marks by reheating and gave glass a shinier finish that was a little closer to that of fine cut crystal.

Simple clear pressed glass articles were combined with other design features and decorating techniques. Pressed glass was made in many colors, flashed, cut occasionally as in simple fluting, cased, or enameled, and might contain applied blown accessories such as handles and feet. All still qualify as pressed glass items, but the quality and dull colors were still far behind cut crystal and Art Glass items; then again, its price wasn't necessarily out of reach for the average American.

Other makers in the late nineteenth and early twentieth centuries in America included the conglomerate United States Glass; George Duncan & Sons; Central Glass Company; Indiana Tumbler & Goblet Company; and many others continued the mass production of pressed glass items. Many of these later pressed patterns were more elaborate, patented, and not as easily copied; a great aid in identification!

ART GLASS

A variety of glass items other than tableware were being made throughout Europe in the nineteenth century, including jugs, water basins, powder jars, jewelry dishes and boxes, toothbrush holders, and soap dishes. The hand-pressing method invented in America was used in England very soon after its initial development. Paperweights were popular in England in the mid-nineteenth century. England and other European countries were the first to spark a revival of cameo cut glass, which had not been made for centuries, since the time of the Islamic glass cutters. John Northwood is credited for the new revival of relief cutting in cameo colors. A blue or plum color cased in white with classic Greek and Roman themes was raised in relief on vases, flasks, plaques, and many other items.

England began and then followed the Art Glass trends in the later nineteenth century. Thomas Webb and his sons were one of the largest producers of Cameo, Burmese, Peach Blow, and a variety of other designs. Several English firms also adopted the cheaper Carnival Glass–making techniques from America in the twentieth century. With the help of the English, Australian glass houses were built and also produced Carnival Glass. The later nineteenth century was a significant period for the entire European community as others joined in.

The biggest impact the French would have in the world of glassmaking was the leadership role in the Art Nouveau movement. Eugène Rousseau and Emile Gallé were the initial French designer-artists and first displayed their fancy glass at the Paris Exposition Universelle. From the time Admiral Perry opened trade with Japan to the West, Rousseau was deeply influenced by Oriental art. This renewed interest in Orientalism in the form of rugs, porcelain, prints, and paintings was also popular in America throughout the Art Nouveau period. Rousseau and Gallé did not limit themselves to Far Eastern influence but rather combined it with traditional German and Italian Renaissance shapes. Gallé more than Rousseau was the inspiration for this period. The new artform not only appeared in glass but in architecture, paintings, posters, book illustrations, furniture, wallpaper, fabric, embroidery, jewelry, and numerous other mediums. Unlike many of the cut glass manufacturers, Gallé signed his works, which sparked others to continue this tradition.

Art Glass was richly ornamental, with little in the way of rules. It was full of originality, displaying crackle effects, metal particles, asymmetrical designs, long sinuous lines, weaving tendrils, flowing rhythms, and wild color effects. Colors and opaqueness were experimented with, and impractical items made of glass had no use except for display and value as a work of art. Whimsies abounded, and such things as insects, animals, fruits, and other recurring themes in nature were all re-created in glass. Rather than typical pretty floral designs, thistle heads, pine cones, and simple plants like wheat were depicted in this glass. There were no set limits or traditions to follow.

Gallé went on to direct the highly acclaimed Nancy School of Art in Nancy, France. The institute dedicated itself to originality, innovation, and artistic achievement in glass. In the 1880s and 1890s, the city of Nancy became the hub of the Art Glass movement in Europe. Enameled, gilded, engraved, and bizarre color effects were all part of Gallé's designs; however, he is most noted for his superb cameo relief creations in glass. Nancy attracted many other noted figures, such as Jean Daum, second only to Gallé in reputation. When Gallé died in 1904, the quality of work in his factory suffered, and many believe that this event was the beginning of the decline of an era.

One other noteworthy French designer and artisan was René Lalique. Lalique began his career as a maker of Art Glass jewelry in the 1890s. He was commissioned by Coty Parfums to produce fancy decorative perfume bottles for Coty's various fragrances. The true artist was now born, and Lalique's famous creations branched into glass sculpture. Figurals, nudes, vases, and even car hood ornaments were formed into frosted crystal works of art. He experimented a little with colors but worked primarily with crystal. Many of his creations contain several separate views, such as a bowl formed by three kneeling nude figures.

Other European countries were part of the Art Nouveau movement. Austrian makers included Johann Lutz, E. Bakalowits, and Moser and Sons; Val St. Lambert was a famous glass city in Belgium; the islands near Venice continued to produce millefiore designs dating back to the thirteenth century; and the most famous American artists, such as Tiffany and Carder, visited Europe to gain firsthand knowledge and ideas of glassmaking trends.

In the midst of America's Brilliant Period (the period following the Early and Middle periods—see "Cut Glass," below), a new form of glass arose.

17

This new Art Nouveau or Art Glass period began in America in the 1880s and lasted well into the early twentieth century. Artists, designers, and other creative people who had not previously worked in glass directed their talents to some of the most unique and spectacular glass objects ever composed. Some authorities have a legitimate argument that the Brilliant Period coupled with the introduction of Art Glass began in America with the Philadelphia Centennial Exhibition in 1876.

As with the expositions taking place in Europe, these events allowed glassmakers to display some of their finest pieces. The Philadelphia event featured a massive cut chandelier and a glass fountain seventeen feet in height. The fountain was an ornamental design with cut crystal prisms lit by 120 gas jets and surmounted by a glass figure of Liberty.

Although the Art Nouveau movement had its beginnings in France with Rousseau and Gallé, America produced its own share of world-class designers. Two of the most famous American Art Glass sculptors were Louis Comfort Tiffany and Frederick Carder.

Tiffany was an American painter who visited Paris in 1889 and observed Gallé's work in person at the Exposition Universelle. He was also the son of the jewelry magnate who had founded Tiffany & Co., the famous jewelry store. Louis Comfort Tiffany began his work in glass by producing stained glass windows without using stains or paints. The color, detail, and illusion were created within the glass itself by plating one layer of glass over another. He broadened his work to include lamps and was one of the first to experiment with iridescent glass. He named his iridescent products Favrile or Tiffany Favrile. The word was derived from the English *fabrile*, which means "belonging to a craftsmen or his craft."

Iridescence is produced by firing on combinations of metallic salts that in turn create a wide variety of coloring effects. Luminous colors and metallic luster produced a silky smooth or delicate patina upon Tiffany's glass. According to Tiffany, his main inspiration was the decayed Roman glass objects discovered in archaeological excavations.

With great success at presenting his works at the World's Exposition in Chicago in 1893, orders poured in and he further expanded his work to other art forms. Tableware, vases, flowers, unique shapes, and many other table items were blown from Tiffany's skilled hands. His designs were never decorated or painted; they were made by combinations of different colored glass during the blowing operation. His goods were displayed throughout Europe, including Paris, at the 1900 Exposition, which in turn inspired young European artists to copy his style.

Frederick Carder was an apprentice of the famous English glass artisan John Northwood. Carder emigrated from Stourbridge, England, and founded the Steuben Glass Works in Corning, New York. Carder created several varieties of lustrous lead glass, such as Aurene, an ornamental iridescent form. He sold Steuben to the Corning Glass Works in 1918 but continued to produce some of the finest crystal forms in the world through 1936 for Corning. Carder's glass was also exhibited at numerous national and international expositions, galleries, and museums.

Many others followed in the footsteps of Tiffany and Carder. So much experimentation took place that America invented more distinctive styles than all of Europe combined. Many American firms copied or attempted to reproduce popular designs of others, and at times, the experimentation led to new creations.

In 1883, Joseph Locke, an Englishmen employed by the New England Glass Company obtained a patent for Amberina. In 1885, another Englishman, Frederick Shirley, patented Burmese for the Mount Washington Glass Company. Burmese products were sent to Queen Victoria of England as gifts, and she was so impressed with the style that she ordered more. Mount Washington shared the formula with Thomas Webb & Sons of England, who also produced Burmese products. In 1886, Shirley also patented Pearl Satin Glass for Mount Washington. In 1887, Locke patented Agata Glass for New England. More patents followed for a huge variety of art styles including Amethyst, Aurora, Cintra, Cluthra, Cranberry, Crown Milano, Custard, Intarsia, Lava, Mercury, Peach Blow, Rubina, Satin, Slag, and Spatter—just to name a few.

Cut Glass

The Brilliant Period of American glassmaking lasted from 1880 to 1915. It was characterized by deep cutting, exceptional brilliance or sparkle, heavy lead crystal formulas, and very elaborate and ornate design. Cut glass is completed by steel or iron wheels revolving in a trough while a stream of water mixed with abrasives drips down upon the wheel from above. This initial process is known as roughing and is responsible for the first cut. Heavier wheels were used to make deeper and sharper cuts. The glass then proceeds to a hard stone wheel, where the rough cut is smoothed out. At this point a polisher would polish it on a softer wooden wheel, and then a buffer would further smooth it out upon a buffing wheel. Buffing was eventually replaced with acid polishing in the 1890s, but true craftsmen argued that acid polishing was inferior, since it wasn't permanent and gradually wore away. Acid polishing also left a somewhat dull finish, obstructing the brilliance of the piece to a small degree.

The aim of a cutter was to remove imperfections and impart facets to capture a good deal of light (the prismatic effect). American inventions improved on cutting. Flat-edged wheels made square-ended cuts, and convex-edged wheels made hollowed cuts. Americans added miter-edged wheels, which made curved or V-shaped cuts. Miter-edged wheels were invented in the later 1870s and freed cutters from the dependence on straight-line cuts. Wheels were made not only of stone and steel but also of copper and carborundum. Electricity, when available, was used to power the wheels as well as to provide the craftsmen with better lighting in which to see by; of course, it may have added more hours to their workday, too! Additional steps were added to the cutting process as finer wheels and milder abrasives made cutting more precise.

Copper wheel cutting or engraving was the end in the evolutionary process for the finest cut glass. Up to 150 wheels of various diameters from the very large down to those the size of a pin were utilized. A copper wheel engraver held the final pattern in his mind without outlining it upon the glass. He then pressed glass objects to the revolving wheel, which instantly cut through or roughened the surface. He rubbed the glass repeatedly with oils, using his fingers, as it was placed on and taken off the wheel. Before electricity, lathes were operated by foot-powered treadles and were somewhat limited in size. An electrically operated lathe made heavier wheels possible, including large diamond-point cutting wheels. It might take weeks, months, and even years to finish a single piece on copper wheels.

Elaborate carving, such as cameo engraving, was also completed on copper wheels. Stone wheels were primarily used for depth, while copper was best for fine detailed work. Copper wheel engravers were compensated more than cutters and were some of the most highly skilled artisans in the glass-making business.

Along with blowers, copper wheel engravers commanded salaries as high as $6.00 a day in the 1880s; common cutters, about $3.50 to $4.00 a day; and ordinary general workmen about $14.00 to $20.00 a week, based on a six-day work week. The higher wages provided incentive to foreign workers to immigrate to America. In Europe, English and Irish glassmakers earned $7.00 to $9.00 per week; Germans and Austrians much less, at $3.00 a week. American wages were typically three to four times greater than their European counterparts. One disadvantage was that European glassmakers produced cheaper glass products in terms of price. Even after a 45 percent tariff was placed on imported glass in 1888, European glassware was still highly competitive. America's own advantages included an abundance of cheap fuel (a problem in Europe) and advanced mechanization.

To make fine cut glass, a quality hand-blown blank was necessary. Many decorating companies purchased blanks of high quality lead glass from major glass companies for their cutters to work. Traditionally, blowers had to be very skilled artisans. Years of training, hard work, and the ability to perform effectively under pressure as well as in poor working conditions were all prerequisites for a successful blower. A blower typically had to work near a blinding furnace with roasting heat, eye-watering smoke, and hands that were constantly scorched and dirtied with coal dust. It was surprising indeed that such exquisite objects could be blown from these stoke hole–like conditions. Under such pressures, the glass blower had to exercise the utmost skill, control, patience, steady nerve, and judgment, all mixed further with creativity and occasional bouts of spontaneity. In short, glass blowing was an art.

There were many other positions in which one could partake in the glassmaking trade. A gatherer was one who gathered a blob of molten glass at the end of a blowpipe, pontil, or gathering iron for the blower. Cutters ordinarily apprenticed for three years at a small salary, usually after completing eight grades of formal education. The best cutters might work up to copper wheel engravers after years of practice.

At the turn of the twentieth century, women held some jobs, though glassmaking was primarily a man's business. Women dusted glass in showrooms and salesrooms, distributed glass to cutters, updated catalogs, made drawings of blanks, waxed the glass before an acid dip, and washed or dried glass before packaging it. A rare enameler or cutter might have been female.

The production of glass itself was not an easy, inexpensive, or safe practice. The basic ingredients of sand, potash, lead for the best crystal, and a few other additions were mixed in a huge clay pot and heated to extreme temperatures. A batch was termed "metal" by chemists, and the best metal batch always contained the highest lead content. Cut glass was usually made with a company's best metal formula.

Molten glass had to be gathered by a worker to press into a mold or simply for the blower to work. Several tools were available, including a pontil, which was used to remove expanded glass objects from the blowing iron; however, it did leave a mark. It was later replaced with a special rod called a gadget. A gadget had a spring clip on its end to grip the foot of a glass piece and hold it while another worker trimmed the rim and applied what finishing touches were needed.

Ovens were important especially those with a special opening called a glory hole. A glory hole was a small-sized opening in the side of the oven where objects could be reheated and reworked without destroying the original shape. A lehr was an annealing oven that toughened glass through gradual cooling. A muffle kiln was a low-temperature oven used for firing on or permanently fusing enamels.

A variety of technical jargon and tools was associated with the glassmaking process. Moil was waste glass left on the blowpipe or pontil. Pucellas were like tongs and were used to grip or grasp glass objects. Arrissing was the process of removing sharp edges from glass. Cracking off involves removing a piece of glass from the pontil by cooling, gently tapping, and then dropping it into a soft sand tray. Fire polishing was the art of reheating objects at the glory hole to remove tool marks.

Glass did not always turn out perfectly and sickness resulted. Sick glass was usually not tempered or annealed properly and showed random cracks, flaking, and possible disintegration. Seeds were tiny air bubbles in glass indicating an underheated furnace or impurities caused by flecks of dirt.

An assortment of other techniques was present in American glass, including a good deal of originality. Cutting was primarily done in geometrical patterns. Pictorial, cameo, and intaglio (heavily engraved) designs were all cut regularly. Acid etching was the process of covering glass with an acid-resistant layer, scratching on a design, and then permanently etching the design with acids. Acid polishing gave cut glass a polished surface by dipping the entire object into a mild solution of sulfuric or hydrofluoric acid. Hand painting and firing on enamels were two additional techniques.

Sandblasting was a distinct American process wherein a design is coated with a protective layer and then the exposed surfaces are sandblasted with a pressurized gun. Trimming with enamels such as silver, gold, and platinum was in use in the early 1900, before World War I. Staining, gilding, monogram imprinting, rubber stamping, and silk screening were other cheaper methods of decorating glass prior to the First World War.

In 1913, a gang-cut wheel was invented in America to make several parallel incisions at once. It made rapid and inexpensive cutting possible, such as cross-hatching and blunt-edged flower petals. For the most part, cut glass was simply that: undecorated crystal except for the elaborate cutting.

The decline of superb cut crystal reached its lowest point as World War I neared. The exclusive market it catered to turned around, as the wealthy preferred more Art Deco styles and European imports. Cheaper glass formulas, labor troubles, increased imports, more and more machine-made glass, and lead needed for the war effort were all factors leading to the end of the Brilliant Period in American glass history.

CARNIVAL GLASS

The problem with Art Glass was the same as that of fine, brilliantly cut crystal. It was too expensive for the average citizen and catered to a very exclusive limited market. An inexpensive pressed substitute did arrive for Tiffany, Steuben, and the English Victorian Glass; and that was Carnival Glass. Nearly all the Carnival Glass in the United States was made between about 1905 and the late 1920s. In the beginning the new pressed glass was not called Carnival but borrowed its name from Tiffany's Favrile and Steuben's Aurene. It soon added other exotic names, such as New Venetian Art, Parisian Art, Aurora, and Art Iridescent.

The techniques of making this glass were also borrowed from the Art Nouveau movement. Color is natural in glass, derived from various oxides present in sand. Ordinarily, iron and common metals produce light green to brown glass. The addition of various metallic oxides, variations in heat and length of time in the furnace, and minor formula changes all produced astounding effects on color. Carnival glass contains a base color, which is the color of the glass before any iridescence is fired upon it. The base color is usually visible on the underside of an iridized glass object.

There were two major groups of colored Carnival Glass. The bright Carnival colors consisted of red, blue, green, purple, amethyst, amber, and marigold. The pastel colors, somewhat rarer, were made up of clear, white, ice green, ice blue, clambroth, lavender, aqua opalescent, peach opalescent, and smoke. Red was the rarest and one of the most expensive to make, since fair amounts of gold oxides were required to produce it. Naturally, red is the most valuable color today and commands very high prices. As the pastel colors are also not as common, they are quite valuable, too.

Marigold was the most popular Carnival color and is the one usually envisioned when one thinks of Carnival Glass. Marigold was an orangish-brown-colored flashing applied to clear glass and then sprayed with iridescence. Pastels usually had clear bases with a very light coating of iridescence. Lavender naturally had a purple tint; aqua, a bluish-green tint; peach, a yellowish-orange tint; smoke, a light gray; and clambroth, a pearly white or light yellow sheen. Other opaque and opalescent shadings were also made. Of all the colors, marigold remains the most abundant and cheapest to acquire.

The glass itself was first manufactured into simple bowls and vases. As its popularity increased, water sets, table sets, punch bowls, berry and ice cream sets, dresser sets with matching cologne bottles, other bottles (wines, whiskey, soda), powder jars, trays, hatpin holders, lamps, paperweights, mugs, beads, advertising items, and souvenir pieces all followed as its popularity exploded.

Unlike fancy Art Glass, Carnival Glass was sold in china shops, in general stores, and by mail order and used as containers for food products such as pickles and mustard. It was the first to be used as prizes for promotional items for tea companies, candy companies, and furniture stores (as Depression Glass would be soon afterward).

Carnival Glass was exported to England and other parts of Europe; it even reached as far as Australia. Several foreign countries began producing it, too, including England, Australia, and Sweden; however, the fad would be a short-lived one.

By the late teens, the demand lessened; and by the early 1920s, the fad had pretty much ended. The modern decor trends of the 1920s had no place for this odd oily glassware. Manufacturers were left with huge inventories, and sold this remaining stock to fairs, bazaars, and carnivals (hence the name "Carnival Glass") at below wholesale prices to rid themselves of it. Those who were stuck with it packed it away until the 1950s.

DEPRESSION GLASS

Despite America's worst Depression, more glass was manufactured during the 1920s and 1930s than at any other time in American history—an amazing feat considering the state of the nation's economy. A great battle ensued in the glass industry between handmade-glass houses and machineware. Hand-cut crystal was far superior in quality, but it was very expensive and lost out to mass-produced machine-made glass on price alone.

The new manufactured glass was flawed and cheaply made, but the price was several times lower than that of handmade glass. Flaws included notice-able air bubbles, slightly inconsistent coloring, and tiny trails of excess glass. These minor flaws do not detract from the value, but chips and cracks render glass virtually worthless. The glass companies that folded during the Depression were those that did not convert to automation. Competing with "2 for a nickel" tumblers and complete sets of tableware that sold for as little as $2 was impossible, especially considering the depressed state of the nation.

Machine-made glassware first appeared on the market in significant quantities following the end of World War I. It sold well, but intense competition and price cutting followed. The profit margin on such products was very low and a higher sales vol-ume was required to sustain such profits; not an easy objective to achieve during an upcoming depression. Cheap handmade imported glass also nearly tripled in the 1920s, providing even more competition for American glass manufacturers.

Despite these difficulties, the Depression era was a banner time for glass production in the United States. More patterns, shapes, and colors were pro-duced in this period than in any other past or pre-sent period in American glass history. Depression Glass includes nearly all glass made in America from the 1920s and 1930s. It was marketed to middle- and working-class Americans, since it sold very inexpensively. The affordable glass could be purchased by the piece or in complete sets. It was available from general or department stores, from factory outlets, by mail order, and wherever house furnishings and kitchenware were sold. Table sets usually included soup and serving bowls, tumblers, plates, and saucers. Added to this could be creamers and sugars, punch sets, vases, candy and cracker jars, water pitchers, butter dishes, dessert dishes, serving platters, salt and pepper shakers, measuring cups, and nearly everything imaginable for the table. Some sets number more than one hundred distinct pieces in the same pattern!

The gaudy art and oily Carnival Glass colors went out of style quickly and were replaced by the simple singular nonopaque colors of the new Depression Glass. Color was added to much of America's gadgets in the Roaring Twenties, from automobiles to kitchen appliances. Colored glass was used as cheap prizes at fairs and exhibitions; complete sets were given away as promotional items with furniture and appliance purchases; and smaller pieces served as bonuses in oatmeal cans, cereal boxes, and household supply containers. With the coming of Depression Glass, glass was so inexpensive that it was no longer a luxury for the well-to-do only. Middle- and working-class Americans purchased it in large quantities.

Colored glass had been in existence for centuries, but the Depression was when it reached its peak of popularity. It was also a time when nearly every company producing glass in America perfected color and further experimented with new combinations. Pink was by far the most common, as evidenced by the slightly lower value of pink Depression Glass. In terms of quantity, green was a close second to pink, followed by amber. Other colors, though somewhat rarer, can also be found in glass of this period. To produce color, metallic as well as nonmetallic elements are necessary. Metals produce the most vibrant and distinct colors, while the nonmetallic agents of phosphorus, selenium, sulfur, and tellurium serve to heighten or intensify specific colors.

The metal manganese produces an amethyst color and is the oldest known, dating back to around 1400 B.C. in Egypt. Copper imparts a light blue and was also utilized by the ancient Egyptians. Cobalt is responsible for the richest, deepest, and most powerful blue coloring. Cobalt blue has long been a staple throughout history. Examples of this beautiful blue glass were found in King Tut's tomb and in stained glass windows of twelfth-century Europe, and cobalt was used extensively for a pottery glaze in both the Tang and Ming dynasties of China.

Lead naturally produces the most outstanding clear crystal; generally, the higher the concentration of lead, the better the clarity and quality of the crystal. Silver also produces crystal, although not as fine or as cheaply as lead. Chromium is responsible for a dark green color that can be heightened by other elements. Iron can be mixed with chromium for a darker green or with sulfur and carbon to produce amber-colored glass. Manufacturers usually avoid sand containing high concentrations of iron, since it tends to make glass a murky green or dull brown. Gold, one of the more expensive coloring agents, imparts a brilliant ruby red color. (Andread Cassius in 1685 is usually credited with this discovery.) Luxurious ruby red glass generally has a higher value than most other colors because of the addition of gold. Rarer colors exist, too, such as a prominent bright yellow produced with uranium and smoky gray-colored glass with nickel.

Aside from coloring, decorating techniques flourished during the Depression years. Some hand etching and copper-wheel engraving survived, but technological advances made it possible for machines to do it more quickly and efficiently. The quality did suffer to some extent, but the labor savings alone more than made up for it. Crackle glass was made by dipping hot glass fresh from a machine mold into cold water to induce numerous cracks over the entire surface of the glass. It was then necessary to reheat the cracked glass and re-form it within the mold. Frosted glass gained somewhat in popularity and consisted of a complete light acid etching over the entire exterior surface of the glass object. The result was a murky light gray coloring.

Machines applied enameling in exactly the right position, which was much quicker than application by hand. Enameled glass was then refired to fuse the paintlike substance permanently. Silk screens were also used to apply patterns, monograms, crests, and so forth. Even decals were fired on some cheaper glassware. Aside from these numerous innovations, the most permanent trademark decorating technique applied to Depression Glass were simple patented patterns pressed into molds by machine.

The popularity of Depression Glass faltered in the late 1930s as Americans tired of the colored glass. A return to crystal as well as new technological advances in ceramics and plastics ended the era of one of the most notable and prolific periods in American glass history. Depression Glass was packed away for years until collectors of the 1960s began reassembling sets. A major resurgence in Depression Glass popularity ever since has produced a multitude of collectors; skyrocketing prices; numerous clubs, books, and newsletters; and simply the most popular glass collecting medium in America.

HOW TO BE AN INSTANT EXPERT IN GLASS COLLECTING

CHAPTER 2

THE GLASS MARKETPLACE

In recent years, glass collectors have proliferated to an astounding degree. Much of this proliferation can be attributed to the rise of reproduction Carnival Glass in the 1960s along with the popularity of Depression Glass. Further proof of this can be found in the amount of new books published, new magazines devoted to glassware, small art glass companies founded, clubs organized, and growing general interest. There are now frequent shows, auctions, and national advertising devoted solely to glass collecting.

For the most part, the hub of the glass world in the United States still centers on the East and Midwest. Historically, factories sprang up in Massachusetts, Pennsylvania, New York, West Virginia, Ohio, and Indiana. With the exception of Bartlett-Collins in Oklahoma, all glass manufactured in America through the Depression years occurred east of the Mississippi River. As a result, prices and availability are adversely affected for those living in the western half of the country.

As the years go by, supply is becoming a problem, which directly influences pricing. Pressed, Cut, Art, and Carnival Glass are generally only available through auctions, choice shows, and exclusive dealers. Depression and even some modern glass is slowly following the trends of its predecessors; however, both are still available through general shows and common dealers.

The best deals on glass are generally the trends followed by dealers; that is, attend numerous auctions, know the value of patterns and styles in order to recognize a good deal when it comes along, answer advertisements in common newspapers by private collectors, look in the rummage/garage sale ads for those selling glassware, join a club in your area of interest, and attend large antique/flea markets.

At nearly every large show there is invariably a wide variety of dealers. Those that specialize in glass will usually sell it at or near the prices listed in popular price guides. It is at the dealers that specialize in other merchandise where the best deals can be found at shows. If these particular dealers have only a few glass items along with a wide variety of other merchandise, they may not know the value of it or may simply offer it at a price more than what they paid for it to realize a profit. In turn, that price may be substantially less than what the piece is worth.

IDENTIFYING GLASS

There is no substitute for a good education. Glass now covers such a wide variety of forms and patterns that it is difficult to study them all. Most collectors focus on a certain category, color, style, manufacturer, or form. The next chapter contains information on fifty of the most popular categories. There is also no substitute for experience in collecting glass. Reading and studying books, visiting museums and art galleries, speaking with dealers and visiting their shops, and attending auctions even if only as a non-bidding participant can all enhance one's knowledge of glassware.

Learn to recognize the *exact* marks and signatures of the various makers, particularly in the items or producers you are most interested in. The simplest of forgeries is that of the mark of a well-known maker applied to what was previously an unmarked object of lesser quality and value. In the next chapter the marks are given along with the patterns and styles where they are known or applied.

Glass that is considered highly collectible dates back to pressed items in the 1820s. Older existing glass products are generally found in museums. Pressed glass is identified by embossed or molded patterns. Ribbing, arches, flutes, bull's-eyes, cables, thumbprints, and other geometrical or lacy designs are all common items on pressed glass. Cut glass often contains similar designs, but higher-grade crystal formulas were used along with designs that were cut by hand rather than applied by machine. As a result, cut glass is sharper, thicker, and much brighter or glossier than pressed glass.

While pressed glass was made by hand-pressing machines, Depression Glass was made by automatic machines. The styles are very similar in that glass is pressed into a mold and the main pattern for it is built into the mold. The main differences are that Depression Glass was made in greater quantities and the majority of it was produced in bright, vivid colors. Older pressed items occasionally were colored, but they were generally duller and easily distinguished from Depression Glass.

Art Glass contains many unique styles, such as color experimentation, opaque and opalescent styles, cameo- or relief-cut styles, gaudy objects and colors, ornamental styles, unique shadings, and a general Victorian Age fondness for ostentation. The most popular object for Art Glass stylings appears on vases. Vases range from a few inches in height to several feet! Most are found in the six-to-twenty-inch range and include such styles as trumpets, jack-in-the-pulpit, lily, tulip, and rose bowls. Other objects include lamps, pitchers, baskets, and paperweights. Art Glass was generally made to be displayed rather than for any practical use.

Carnival Glass was originally considered as a cheap version of Art Glass. Carnival Glass was pressed into molds and then sprayed with metallic salts to produce the oily surface coloring. Carnival Glass is usually fairly easy to identify, but it can be confused with more modern and reproduction iridescent forms. To make matters worse, some Depression Glass included light marigold iridescent forms. Carnival Glass had a short history and was made only from the turn of the century until the mid-1920s.

Other glass objects that have found their way into the hands of collectors are more specific, which simplifies identification. These might include such collectibles as fruit jars, bottles, character glass, Christmas glass, Disney glass, Fire King ovenware, marbles, paperweights, souvenir glass, and thimbles.

PRICING

With the huge variety of glass shows, numerous auctions, and national advertising, prices are becoming more standardized for glass collectibles. The values mentioned in the next chapter should serve as a general guide only. They are not intended to set prices; rather, they are determined from hundreds of shows, dealers, auctions, mail order listings, experts in the field, and private collectors. Neither the author nor the publisher assumes responsibility for any losses that might possibly be incurred as a result of using them. The purpose of pricing information in this book is to provide general guidelines for common collectible glassware.

Prices listed in this book are based on glass in excellent condition. Glass that is chipped, heavily scratched, cracked, poorly finished, or with other major problems has very little value. Age, condition, demand, availability, and other factors are directly relevant to pricing. Take special note that dealers pay only about half of the quoted prices. The pricing information is based on retail prices that collectors expect to pay at dealers and shops.

Glass objects of rarity and significant value are rarely sold for a fraction of their actual worth. Carder, Steuben, Tiffany, Gallé, etc., are simply not found at flea markets and rummage sales. The majority of fancy glass products in the past were purchased almost exclusively by the upper echelons of society. On the flip side, do not get caught up in bidding wars at auctions in the heat of the moment. At times, collectors searching for a matching or highly desirable piece may pay an exorbitant price; of course, if it is you who have found the piece of your dreams, it is, after all, your money! Visiting a few galleries, signing up on "Want Lists" from specific dealers, and some traveling may get you the piece you are looking for without excessive bidding.

CONDITION OF GLASS

The condition of glass, much like the pricing, differs between the categories. There is simply no other category of glass that requires as much attention as Art Glass. Pieces that run into the thousands and even the hundreds of thousands deserve extremely careful attention.

The tiniest chip or crack; any missing portion; any part that is repaired or reground; discoloration; staining; internal bubbles that have burst; variations in cutting, engraving, or enameling; or any problem, no matter how minor, should at the very least reduce the prices of fancy art glass. The only exception would be for a few minor scratches on the underside of the base on which the object rests.

A knowledgeable and reputable dealer is essential when purchasing. A dealer should stand by the work, which might turn out to be a reproduction or even a fake. A signed certificate of authenticity should pose no difficulty from a dealer, auction house, or similar organization. Get a second opinion if there is the least bit of doubt. Museum personnel, licensed appraisers, or others with knowledge in the field should be called upon.

Older glass will usually have some telltale sign of wear. A slight fading that does not detract from the item's overall appearance may be evident. Tiny or random scratches on the base are common for Art Glass; most are present simply because the object has stood in one place for so long. A piece that appears brand-new just might be!

No matter how close it comes, the color of reproduction glassware always seems to differ slightly or to some larger degree from the originals, mostly because of the original formulas and ingredients utilized in the glassmaking process. Sand, lead, and other additives are nearly impossible to duplicate through the decades, especially when they are obtained from different sources or regions. The raw materials and sandbanks of a hundred years ago no longer exist in some parts of the country. The slightest variation in color, shade, or hue from known examples can clue one to the existence of a reproduction.

Like Art Glass, cut glass was also an exclusive product for the wealthy. Because of the extremely heavy lead content as well as the extensive hand cutting, hand engraving, and hand polishing involved, reproductions of the original cut patterns have not been made using these methods. Because of the thick, heavy cuts, some lead cut glass has a thickness that exceeds ½ inch! One of the biggest mistakes people make is the assumption that thick glass is strong and durable. Cut glass is fragile because cutting weakens the glass structurally, especially deeper and asymmetrical cutting.

Quality and condition are the two most prevalent factors when inspecting cut glass. Light refraction—a natural crystal gleam is far superior to a cheaper acid finish; uniform weight, balance, and thickness; true symmetrical cuts that are sharp and precise; a lack of cloudiness; and a resonating bell-like sound when tapped with a fingernail are all determining factors of quality. Nicks, tiny chips, discoloration, a dull finish, and scratches all reduce the value of fine cut glass. Any major flaws, such as heavy scratching or chipping, render the object virtually worthless.

Originally, Carnival Glass was produced as a cheap substitute for Art Glass; however, prices for some Carnival Glass have easily reached the Art Glass level. Less expensive common items should be given the same general visual and hand inspection as all glassware. The rare and incredibly valuable items such as red Carnival should follow the careful procedures as mentioned under Art Glass.

Since Carnival Glass is characterized by an iridescent metal flashing, that is the one area of inspection that differentiates it from most other glassware. The iridization should flow smoothly and consistently over the entire object. Gaps, discolorations, dull areas from excessive wear, or any incomplete flashing reduces the price. The base color in most pieces should be visible only on the underside; if it can be viewed in significant areas or portions on the outside, it may be a sign that the iridization has worn off or was incomplete.

Reproductions pose problems in Carnival Glass. Some iridized Depression Glass and later iridized examples resemble the original Carnival designs. Naturally, those that cause the most severe problems are new pieces made in the original molds. Fortunately, there are some manufacturers, such as Imperial, who marked the new wares ("IG") to distinguish them from the old.

Pressed patterns are the oldest styles of glass priced in this guide. They are for the most part nineteenth-century hand-pressed items that vary a good deal in consistency. The results are objects with wide variations in shape, pattern, type, and general formula. Ribbing may be thicker or thinner; vines may be single or double; gridding or checkering may be narrow or wide; and even clear glass tends to acquire a pale purple tinge with age. Manganese in the basic formula is responsible for amethyst coloring; a little too much coupled with prolonged exposure to the sun is responsible for this tinting.

Beware of tinging as well as serious flaws within old pattern glass. Some clear Depression patterns and reproductions are at times confused with older and more valuable pressed designs. Thinner examples can be quite fragile, but for the most part the formulas used in pressed glass have held together well. One last item of note is to look out for irregular, out-of-balance, or slightly stretched pieces, or ones that appear off-center, including the pattern.

In no other category is the chip as much of a factor as in Depression Glass. As a rule, most Depression Glass was mass-produced cheaply in machines in great quantities for the general public. Through constant everyday use coupled with the thinner designs that were no longer hand-cut, chipping is a severe problem with Depression Glass. Feet, rims, lids, handles, joints, and so on should all be carefully inspected for chips. Run your finger around these places with your eyes closed to discover chips by touch.

Minor flaws such as an occasional tiny air bubble, slight inconsistent coloring from piece to piece, and tiny trails of excess glass do not detract from the value of Depression Glass. A typical Depression mold might last for thousands of machine pressings, and it was impossible to match perfectly batch after batch of color. As a result, it is possible to accumulate a matching patterned set of more than fifty pieces that vary slightly in color. Major flaws such as excess scratching, large trails of glass, rough mold lines, chips, and missing pattern designs render Depression Glass virtually worthless.

Reproductions pose a few difficulties; however, there appear to be major differences in the new versions. The most prevalent difference is color. New reproduction colors appear washed out, dull, and not as attractive as the originals. Other differences involve dimensions and new colors that were not produced in the older original versions.

There is little to report on glass produced within the last fifty years or so. In short, it should be in nothing less than new condition. Occasionally, enameling on cheaper advertising or character glass may fade or scratch easily, but if it is abundantly available, less than perfect items should be passed over unless they are highly desired and quite scarce. Even brand new items should be inspected for any damage or flaws that may have occurred in the manufacture, transport, shipping, or simply from being moved around constantly upon display shelves.

CARE OF GLASS

There have been horror stories of glass shattering or spontaneously breaking from changes in temperature, sitting in one place for too long, or simple movement. Some of it is grounded in myth; however, glass does require some minimal care. Machine and pressed glasswares are generally sturdy and were designed for utilitarian purposes. Fancier items such as Art Glass were designed for display purposes as true objets d'art.

Glass will break from sudden temperature changes. Much can depend on how fragile the piece in question is. A warm piece of glass at room temperature may break if suddenly exposed to cold weather outside. When transported, glass should be carefully wrapped and then remain wrapped where it has been transported for several hours until it gradually adjusts to the new temperature. Milk glass has been known to be especially vulnerable to temperature.

Never wash glassware until it has adjusted to room temperature. Use lukewarm or warm water, for scalding-hot water can easily destroy glass. Mild nonabrasive cleaning solutions should be used only on ordinary pressed wares such as Depression Glass. Some art forms should not be washed with water at all! Anything beyond dusting may affect the finish.

Exposing older lead crystal to direct sunlight for lengthy periods can cause the manganese to react and turn the object a light shade of purple. Collectible glass is best stored in sturdy cabinets or on well-secured shelves away from direct sunlight. Occasionally, it should be cleaned and moved. There is sometimes a debate among chemists as to whether glass is a liquid or a solid. It appears to be a solid, but some low-quality forms have been known to run over time. Check out an old abandoned home sometime and observe any remaining windows. Occasionally, you will find glass that has thickened and bulged at the bottom. Fortunately, the effect of gravity is a rarity in collectible glass; however, sitting in one spot for decades may cause a gradual run over time.

Older glass was not designed for the high pressure and extreme temperatures of dishwashers. Likewise, microwave use is not recommended either, even though it has been proven that the lead in glass does not react to microwave energy. New glass products are acceptable for microwave use as long as it is recommended by the manufacturer; older items are not!

History has shown that glass has survived the test of time. Look in the major museums such as the Corning Museum of Glass or the Chrysler Museum and you will find pieces that have survived for centuries. With a little careful attention, your pieces will last as well.

CHAPTER 3

GLASS COLLECTOR CATEGORIES FROM A TO Z

THE FIFTY MOST POPULAR GLASS COLLECTIBLE CATEGORIES

Advertising Glass

Advertising was first applied to bottles but soon became fashionable with jars, drinking glasses, mugs, and a variety of other objects. Advertising glass was made by most major glass companies operating in America in the nineteenth as well as the early twentieth century. The most collectible items include those in colors such as cobalt blue, emerald green, Carnival styles, and even brown. Colored items including general Carnival Glass colors with advertising typically sell from around $75 to $100 for more common items like mugs and plates up to several hundred dollars for rarer colors like Carnival amethyst or purple.

Inexpensive advertising items that sell for less than $25 include ashtrays, banks, mugs,

Photo by Robin Rainwater

*Blue Carnival
Souvenir Mug*

trays, tumblers, and measuring cups. Keep an eye
out for Planter's Peanut jars, since some are reproductions. The most desirable are the older emerald
green and cobalt blue versions that sell in the $100
to $200 range. The newer ones include clear glass
and a darker forest green. The new peanut jars
retail for about $25 to $35. Refer to the "Bottles"
and "Shot glasses" headings in this chapter for
more information.

Amberina Art Glass

Amberina is a single-layered style of glass created
by the New England Glass Company in 1883.
Joseph Locke was responsible for much of its development. Amberina is characterized by an amber
color at the bottom of an object that gradually
shades into red at the top. The shading could very
well change from object to object. The red might
be a brilliant ruby red or a deep violet sometimes
referred to as fuchsia. Gold was often mixed with
the transparent amber to produce the red coloring
affect.

The New England Glass Company placed a

New England Glass Works Paper Label

high-quality vibrantly colored thick Amberina plating on some of its wares. These particular items are very rare and valuable. Amberina was made in both art objects and functional tableware. The style was continued under Edward Libbey when he purchased the company and moved it to Toledo, Ohio. Both the New England Glass Works and Libbey can be found on many examples. Amberina was most popular in the 1880s and was revived by Libbey from 1917 to 1920, but it did not do well and was discontinued.

In the meantime, Libbey did sell some patent rights, including Amberina, to others, such as Tiffany and Mount Washington. Varieties of Amberina have been reproduced by several companies and individuals. Reproductions exist, too, as well as less valuable flashed-on and enameled examples. Flashed-on and enameled items usually include metal oxides that produce an iridescent finish or enamel that flecks or eventually peels. The original Amberina has no such iridescence and was rarely enameled.

The original pieces typically sell for several hundred dollars. The most highly desirable plated Amberina items sell for several thousand dollars. Look for the New England or Libbey trademarks on some original Amberina products.

Animals

Animals made of glass became popular in the early twentieth century, and that popularity has only increased since. Early items included covered and open dishes such as swans and roosters. Early twentieth-century manufacturers include Heisey, Fosto-

Gibson Glass

Boyd Crystal Art Glass

*Sabino 1990s
Advertisement*

ria, Duncan & Miller, New Martinsville, and Cambridge. The early crystal Heisey animals are the most valuable today and typically sell for several hundred dollars. Duncan & Miller's and New Martinsville's are not far behind in price. Cambridge produced animals up into the 1950s and was one of the first to employ wide use of color in the manufacture of them. Cambridge was famous for swans, and the larger birds sell for $100 to $300, depending on the color.

A new glass animal collector craze began with animals in the early 1980s with such companies as Boyd, Guernsey, Gibson, Pisello, Summit, Sabino, and a variety of other classic companies such as Baccarat, Waterford, and Steuben. Boyd produces many limited pieces in specific color designs, including Carnival or iridescent, slag, satin, and swirls. Already some of Boyd's creations that retailed for $6 to $8 in the 1980s are selling for over $20. Steuben makes only crystal; however, that crystal is the finest in the world and retails for a minimum of $150. Sabino's frosted and lightly iridized animals sell in the $35 to $50 range. For a unique piece, track down Baccarat's Loch Ness monster, which comes in four separate pieces and retails for about $300.

Avon Glass Collectibles

Though not a maker of glass products, Avon has commissioned hundreds of products since the late 1920s. Popular modern sets that are issued a piece at a time (two or three annually) include the ruby red Cape Cod pattern, the etched Hummingbird crystal

Avon commission (Fostoria Coin Glass). Cameo portrait of either George or Martha Washington.

Photo by Robin Rainwater

pattern (made in France), and even some coin glass and other glass products made by Fostoria.

The majority of Avon products sell in the $10 to $30 range; however, the dark amber chess set in its entirety is worth about $500. The chess pieces are actually silverplated caps on amber bottles. The coin glass items are in cobalt blue and contain a pair of goblets with medallions of George and Martha Washington along with a small pitcher containing a medallion of Mount Vernon. Coin glass items sell for about $25 each.

Baskets

Glass baskets date back at least to seventeenth-century Germany but were far more popular in the eighteenth century. The famous Venetian makers on Murano as well as artisans in the Netherlands and Spain produced them in some quantity in the eighteenth century. The popularity of baskets car-

Gibson Ad

45

ried over to America as well, and glass manufacturers in America included Heisey, Cambridge, Tiffany, and, most recently, Fenton.

Glass baskets are an art form. Unlike wicker or wooden baskets, most glass baskets were utilized as display pieces to hold floral arrangements, candles, or potpourri. A few were designed for the table to hold such foods as salt, nuts, sugar, and jelly. Occasionally, baskets can be found with matching spoons for dispensing certain foods such as jelly.

Baskets comes in all shapes, sizes, and colors. Simple pressed crystal or lime glass items sell for about $20 to $25. Cut crystal baskets can be priced as high as $1,000 depending on the size, cutting, and engraving. Fancy Art Glass baskets in various shaded, spattered, and applied color patterns typically sell in the $100 to $300 range. Even newer items such as Fenton's various colored and opalescent designs retail in the $50 range.

Blenko Glass Co.

Blenko Glass

The Blenko Glass Company was founded by English immigrant William J. Blenko in 1922. He began as a hand producer of stained glass windows, but the company later switched to more

1966 Blenko Glass Advertisement

contemporary Art Glass forms. Blenko products consist of bright vibrant colors along with some art styles such as crackling, bubbling, and unique shapes. Blenko pieces are usually reasonably priced, in the $20 to $40 range.

Bohemian Glass

Bohemia is an area in Europe that adjoins Bavaria and Silesia, now mostly part of the Czech Republic. Functional glass such as windows and drinking glasses date as far back as the late fourteenth century in this area. It was not until the sixteenth and late seventeenth centuries that a unique recognizable style of glass was attributed to this area. The original Bohemian glass was characterized by heavy stone engraving overlaid with colored glass. A later design included the cutting of two layers of colored glass. The object was then gilded or enameled.

Bohemian Glass Advertisement—1980s

Individual items can be difficult to date because the glass has been continuously produced for more than three hundred years by several manufacturers. Similar products made in Austria and Germany add to the confusion. Popular products include engraved crystal and colored beakers, flasks, decanters, steins, vases, plates, and tumblers. Most contain mountains, forests, hunting themes, and other scenes of nature. Prices generally range from about $100 for smaller pieces such as wineglasses and tumblers up to several hundred for more elaborately engraved pieces.

Boston & Sandwich Glass

One of America's early successful firms, Boston & Sandwich was noted most for Sandwich or pressed

Boston & Sandwich Vase

Photo by Robin Rainwater

glass, from which its name is derived. It manufactured large amounts of this new hand-pressed glass but occasionally created objets d'art in the form of lacy glass in the French style, paperweights, opal wares, engraved glass, and probably its most famous product, Mary Gregory glass.

Mary Gregory glass is characterized by crystal and colored glassware (most commonly pastel pink) decorated with white enameled designs of one or more boys and/or girls playing in Victorian scenes. Mary Gregory actually worked as a decorator for the Boston & Sandwich Glass Company from 1870 to 1880, but it is not known whether or not she painted the glass of her namesake.

Refer to the "Pressed Glass" section for pricing on those items. Generally, colored Art Glass products made by Boston & Sandwich sell for $100 to $200 for smaller items such as tumblers and bowls, while fancy vases, candlesticks, and paperweights sell for several hundred dollars. Mary Gregory items are usually priced in the $150 to $500 range, depending on how elaborate the piece is. Beware of recent Czechoslovakian Mary Gregory reproductions made in the 1970s and 1980s.

Bottles

Bottles cover a wide range of categories, styles, and manufacturers. Those old brown or dark amber beer bottles from the past fifty years are still reasonably priced in the $10 to $50 range. Look for other colors, too, such as aqua, blue, and green. Bitters' or medicine bottles are older, rarer, and often contain etched or molded (embossed) advertising.

A few smaller and common bitters bottles may be priced as inexpensively as beer bottles; however, the vast majority are in the $50 to $200 range. A few rare colors and unique shapes have been known to sell in excess of $1,000.

Perfume bottles with ordinary or common advertising may sell for as little as $5, while fancy French art designs such as Lalique or Baccarat sell for several hundred. Milk bottles are available in the thousands, and those advertised with dairy names typically sell in the $10 to $25 range.

The largest category of bottles is a toss up between soda pop and whiskey. Nineteenth- and even eighteenth-century whiskey bottles made of colored glass often sell for more than $1,000. Soda pop bottles, particularly those with national advertising such as Coca-Cola and Pepsi, typically sell in the $10 to $50 range, while a few rare items sell for several hundred.

Cambridge Glass

The Cambridge Glass Company was established in Cambridge, Ohio, in the early 1900s and was a major producer of crystal products up to the 1950s, when the factory closed. Many Cambridge products were cut and included such designs as stars, swirls, wreaths, squares, and other etchings. The majority of Cambridge's products were made for the table and include bowls, plates, tumblers, and cocktail glasses.

Cambridge products are generally priced from as low as $5 for such items as shot glasses, juice tumblers, and saucers to as high as $100 for more

Cambridge Glass Co.

elaborate pieces such as decanters and buffet sets (plate, divided bowl, and ladles). One of Cambridge's most collectible patterns is the Square series produced shortly before Cambridge went out of business. Pieces in this pattern generally have a square shape or design at the base. Cambridge produced square pieces in crystal only; however, when it closed, the Imperial Glass Company acquired the molds and produced several square pieces in red and black. Colored square pieces generally sell for about one and a half times those of crystal.

Candlewick

Candlewick is a huge set that was first introduced in 1936 by the Imperial Glass Corporation. It was made continuously from 1936 until Imperial closed in 1982. There are well over 600 separate items made in the Candlewick design. Candlewick is unmarked except for paper labels, which are naturally removed; however, it is easily identified by beaded crystal stems, handles, and rims. The name of the pattern comes from the tufted needlework of pioneer women, which the basic design resembles.

For the most part, Candlewick was produced in crystal; however, a few items were made in blue, red, amber, green, black, amethyst, pink, and yellow. Some Candlewick items were decorated in silver, gold, chrome, brass, or wood. Recent reproductions have been a problem, since the original molds were sold to a variety of different companies. Some new pieces are marked (e.g., the "B" in a diamond signifying Boyd), while others are not. Unmarked pieces tend to be somewhat heavier than the originals and have ground bottoms.

The value of Candlewick is a measure of what most major patterns represent: the larger the piece, the larger the price. Exceptions include rare pieces. In Candlewick, prices for smaller items are in the $10 to $30 range and include regular plates and bowls,

1911

1913

1914

1921

spoons, trays, tumblers, and goblets. Larger and rarer pieces typically sell for more, such as baskets, large serving bowls, candle holders, covered jars, egg plates, ice tubs, serving pitchers, platters, and vases. The most valuable set is probably the punch bowl with matching base plate, cups, and ladle. These sets now sell in excess of $300.

Canning Jars

Canning jars are also known as fruit jars or even Mason jars. They are designed to preserve food, and although they have been made in the millions for well over a century, there exists many off brands and rare colors from the nineteenth and early twentieth centuries that are quite valuable today. Nearly all jars have mold embossed writing and/or designs.

Note that the dates on certain jars (e.g., "Patented November 30, 1858") refer to the patent date, not the actual age of the jar. Common clear and bluish-green or aqua jars may sell for only a few dollars, but rarer colors such as green, amethyst, and amber sell from $20 to $100. A rare cobalt blue Canton two-quart jar from the late nineteenth century recently sold for more than $2,000!

Carnival Glass

Carnival Glass is pressed glassware with a fired-on iridescent finish made in the United States from about 1905 to the late 1920s. A little Carnival Glass was also produced in England and Australia. There were five major companies that produced the majority of Carnival Glass in America: the Fenton Art Glass Co. of Williamstown, West Virginia; the Imperial Glass Corporation of Bellaire, Ohio; the Millersburg Glass Company of Millersburg, Ohio; the Northwood Glass Company of Wheeling, West Virginia; and the Dugan Glass Company of Indiana, Pennsylvania. A few other companies that produced limited amounts of Carnival Glass included Cambridge, Jenkins, Heisey, Indiana, Federal, Fostoria, McKee-Jeannette, Westmoreland, and U.S. Glass.

Noted individuals were Frank and John Fenton, who founded Fenton, John also went on, with another brother, Robert, to establish Millersburg. Jacob Rosenthal was also employed by the Fentons and developed many Carnival Glass formulas. Edward Muhleman founded Imperial, while Harry Northwood (son of English glass artisan John Northwood) established Northwood. Harry Northwood's managers Thomas E. Dugan and W. G. Minnemeyer went on to form the Dugan Glass Company.

Northwood Glass Co.

Fenton and Imperial both made iridescent products in the modern era. Nearly all of Fenton's recent works are easily distinguished from the older versions, and Fenton continues in operation today. Imperial began reproducing Carnival Glass in the early 1960s, using some of the original molds; however, the new glass is marked "IG" on the base or bottom. Imperial survived several rough moments in the past but finally shut down for good in 1982.

Carnival Water Set

Photo by Robin Rainwater

There are two major groups of colored Carnival Glass. The bright Carnival colors are red, blue, green, purple, amethyst, amber, and marigold. The pastel colors are somewhat rarer and comprise clear, white, ice green, ice blue, clambroth, lavender, aqua opalescent, peach opalescent, and smoke. Red is the rarest and was one of the most expensive to make, since fair amounts of gold oxides were required to produce it. Naturally, red is the most valuable color today and commands very high prices. The pastel colors are also not as common and are quite valuable, too.

Item	Marigold	Bright Colors	Pastels	Red
Bowls, 5"–6"	$30	$40	$60	$500
Bowls, 7"–9"	50	60	75	750
Bowls, over 9"	65	75	100	1000
Butter dish with cover	200	225	300	2500
Candlestick	100	150	250	1000
Covered cookie or candy jar	250	300	750	2500
Creamer and sugar (set)	125	175	350	2000
Cup or mug	100	150	200	1000
Decanter	1000	1250	1500	2500
Pitcher, water	225	350	600	5000
Plate, up to 6"	75	125	200	500
Plate, over 6"	100	150	250	750
Punch bowl with base	400	500	5000	10000
Tumbler, up to 12 oz.	65	80	125	750
Tumbler, over 12 oz.	75	100	175	1000

Marigold is the most popular Carnival color and is the one usually envisioned when one thinks of Carnival Glass. Marigold was an orangish-brown colored flashing applied to clear glass and then sprayed with iridescence. Pastels usually have clear bases with a very light coating of iridescence. Lavender naturally has a purple tint; aqua, a bluish-green tint; peach, a yellowish-orange tint; smoke, a light gray; and clambroth, a pearly white or light yellow sheen. Other opaque and opalescent shadings were also made Out of all the colors, marigold remains the most abundant and cheapest to acquire.

The glass itself was first manufactured into simple bowls and vases. As its popularity increased, water sets, table sets, punch bowls, berry and ice cream sets, dresser sets with matching cologne bottles, other bottles (wines, whiskey, soda), powder jars, trays, hatpin holders, lamps, paperweights, mugs, beads, advertising items, and souvenir pieces all followed. On the previous page is a simple chart for the quick pricing of general Carnival glass. Keep in mind that there are many rare patterns and designs that do not fall into this pricing.

Character Glass

Character glass is a fairly broad category. It refers to cartoon characters, comic book heroes and heroines, movie stars, and other figures that are primarily machine enameled, transfer-labeled, or fired on with decals. A transfer label is one that is printed on a paper backing and then permanently fixed to glass by heating at a high temperature. Designs are most often applied to drinking tumblers and are available in modern times at fast-food restaurants. Many are sponsored by the giants of the soft drink industry such as Coca-Cola and Pepsi.

Character glass has its origins in 1937, when Libbey won a contract with Walt Disney to produce eight separate glass cottage cheese containers enameled with Snow White and the Seven Dwarfs. The complete set of eight now sells for around $150.

Swanky Swigs soon followed, which were small Kraft cheese spread containers with an enameled design or pattern. By soaking the label off, one could transform the jars into juice glasses or drinking tumblers. Swanky Swigs sell in the $5 to $10 range.

Fast-food tumblers really took off in the 1970s, and hundreds of designs have been produced since. Most sell in the $5 to $10 range; these include the B.C. Comics, California Raisins, Care Bears, Alvin and the Chipmunks, Flintstones, Garfield (includes glass mugs too), Muppets, McDonald's, Smurfs, Tom and Jerry, and Looney Tunes. The more valuable, in the $15 to $20 range, include Bullwinkle and Rocky, the Pepsi Hanna Barbera 1977 collector series (e.g., Flintstones, Scooby Do, Jetsons), Star Wars, the cartoon superheroes (e.g., Superman, Batman, Wonderwoman), and Underdog. For the rare seventies, try to find the original *Star Trek* and *Star Trek* cartoon series tumblers sponsored by Dr. Pepper. These tumblers sell for about $50.

Christmas Glass

Over the last two decades, hand-blown and spun glass Christmas ornaments have been produced in ever increasing quantities and styles. Spun glass is thin glass threading that was originally spun by hand on a revolving wheel. Much of it is done by machine today; however, in countries like Taiwan and China, spun glass ornaments are still fashioned on small mechanical wheels.

Generally, the larger the ornament, the higher the value. Such items in the 1-inch to 3-inch range sell for a few dollars. The dimension could refer to length or height and may include such things as angels, hearts, bells, icicles, candles, candy canes, stars, and sleds. The more elaborate spun glass ornaments may include a balloon with attached basket, a gazebo with a dancing couple inside, a carousel with three or four horses, a fire or train engine, a wishing well with detachable basket, and an antique sewing machine complete with table. These items are already selling for $20 to $25.

Over the past few years, several companies are expanding into the ornament business. Steuben recently began producing a crystal star and pine cone that sell for $95 each. Goebel, a German company, makes cut glass bells for about $10. Lenox makes flat glass ornaments with years and stars that sell for around $10. Many companies such as Disney have commissioned ornaments with their characters on them as well.

Coca-Cola Glass Collectibles

You will find books as well as a category in most major antique guides for Coca-Cola–related items, and glass is no exception. Coca-Cola was first produced in Atlanta, Georgia, in 1886 and since then has become a major American icon. Just having the patented Coca-Cola or Coke trademarks will often double or triple the price of ordinary collectible items.

Naturally, the most popular medium for Coca-Cola glass items is bottles. Over the past fifty years, more than one thousand commemorative Coca-Cola bottles have been issued. These feature music legends, presidents, sports stars and coaches, and commemorative events such as centennials, and so on. A few, such as the Ty Cobb 1983 Georgia Peach bottle and the Jimmy Carter 1976 bottle already sell in excess of $100. Nineteenth-century

1900–1920 Coca-Cola bottles. The two in the center are amber.

and early-twentieth-century colored bottles are rare and valuable, too, and also sell for over $100. An important note is that newer bottles should be full and sealed; if not, their value is reduced by as much as 50 percent.

Other Coca-Cola glass items include shot glasses issued in 1969 and annually from 1977 to 1988. Shot glasses are worth $15 to $20. Coca-Cola ashtrays sell for about $25; drinking glasses or tumblers, from $10 to $20; and turn-of-the-century mirrors, for around $300.

Crackle Glass

The crackle effect on glass is produced by plunging a hot glass object into lukewarm or cool water to induce a wide variety of cracks. The object is then refired and often coated to cover the cracks. Crackle glass was first experimented with in the late nineteenth century and became popular in both the Carnival and Depression Glass eras with many companies.

Carnival crackle items were produced in marigold, green, and purple and generally sell for less than comparable items produced in other patterns. Common items like cups, tumblers, creamers and sugars, bowls, and plates sell in the $20 to $30 range, while more elaborate items like pitchers and punch bowls sell in the $75 to $125 range. Depression crackle pieces were usually made in pink, green, and amber and sell for about a third less than the Carnival pieces. As usual, crystal pieces sell for about half the price of their color counterparts, and crackle items are no exception.

Cranberry Glass

Cranberry is sometimes referred to as a light ruby or rose red colored glass. It is a transparent glass the color of dark pink or light red cranberries. It was created by adding tiny amounts of gold oxide as the primary coloring agent. Larger amounts of gold produce a darker true ruby red. Cranberry colored glass is one of the oldest forms of Art Glass produced in America and dates back to the 1820s. Cranberry glass was a popular item with many noteworthy glass and decorating companies including T. B. Clark, T. G. Hawkes, Mount Washington, New England, Northwood, and Steuben.

Common cranberry items such as bowls, creamers and sugars, plates, salt and pepper shaker sets, toothpick holders, tumblers, and vases generally sell in the $100 to $200 range. More elaborate pieces such as water pitchers, decanters, epergnes, and lamps sell for much more.

Beware of cheaper flashed, coated, and stained articles in the identical or similar color. They chip and scratch more easily if the color is not consistent throughout the entire glass, inside and out. Cranberry has been reproduced by several modern companies in a wide variety of items.

Custard Glass

"Custard" refers to the milky white to deep yellow opaque coloring like that of custard pudding. It is sometimes referred to as Buttermilk because the color also resembles yellow buttermilk. Uranium salts are often added to produce a vibrant yellow opalescence that is very mildly radioactive (safe for one to handle!) and reacts to black light.

Common custard items are priced similarly to the cranberry pieces above ($100 to $200), while the larger and more intricately designed pieces naturally sell for more. As with most Art Glass, a variety of decorations and colors were applied to the base custard color. These include a flashing or an enameling of blue, brown, green, pink, red, and even gold gilding or painting. Flower enameling is the most common, but the basic glass itself was produced in numerous patterns by a host of companies. Northwood is recognized as the most prolific producer of custard glass, but a good deal was also made by Adams, Cambridge, Diamond, Dugan, Fenton, Greenberg, Heisey, Jefferson, LaBelle, McKee, and many others.

Cut Glass

Heavy crystal or flint glass is used in the process of producing cut glass. The term "flint" is an American one and is applied to quality lead crystal made during the Brilliant Period (1880–1915). At one time glass experimenters used powdered flint as a substitute for lead oxides. Cut glass is produced by hand-cutting patterns into glass blanks with the use of grinding wheels and abrasives. A blank is simply an uncut piece of glass such as a bowl or vase that has been specifically made of heavy lead glassware. Many decorating and cutting companies purchased blanks from others.

Some of the biggest names in the cut glass world included Libbey, T. G. Hawkes, C. Dorflinger, Mount Washington/Pairpoint, John Hoare, T. B. Clark, H. P. Sinclaire, and Tuthill. Hundreds of cut glass patterns were made, and though many were patented, they were still copied or similar variations of them were produced by others. There were also many common designs or combinations shared by all, including rosettes, hobstars, fans, strawberry diamonds, geometric cuts, flutes, buzz-stars, crosshatching, blocks, and hobnails. Fortunately, more distinct marks and signatures were applied to cut glass products than to any other category of glass.

The glass itself, because of its expense, was produced mostly in functional tableware primarily for

Mount Washington Glass Works Cut Glass Advertisement

Almy & Thomas

J. Hoare & Co.

C. G. Alford & Co.

M. J. Averback

Abraham & Straus Inc.

Pitkin & Brooks

J. D. Bergen Co.

T. B. Clark & Co.

H. P. Sinclaire & Co.

C. Dorflinger & Sons

Meridien Cut Glass Co.

L. Straus & Sons

Crown Cut Glass Co.

Maple City Glass Co.

Tuthill Cut Glass Co.

Taylor Brothers Co.

O.F. Eggington Co.

T. G. Hawkes & Co.

the privileged classes. Such items as bowls, butter dishes, goblets, compotes, decanters, trays, nappies, serving pitchers, tumblers, plates, and vases are common cut glass items. Much of cut glass is marked, so look for signatures, especially those that cannot be felt by your finger. Reproductions usually have slightly raised acid-etched identification marks or signatures that can be felt with your finger. Keep in mind that there are also many quality pieces that were not signed. Look for deep, sharp cuts as well as a lustrous finish.

Listed below is a simple chart for the quick pricing of common cut glass items. Generally, the bigger the piece, the higher the price. Keep in mind that there are many rare patterns and designs that do not fall into this pricing.

Item	Price Range
Bowls, up to 5″	$100-150
Bowls, 6″–7″	125–175
Bowls, 8″–9″	150–200
Bowls, over 9″	200–300
Butter dish with cover	500–750
Candlestick	175–225
Creamer and sugar (set)	300–400
Decanter with cut stopper	400–500
Goblet	125–175
Nappy (see bowls)	
Pitcher, milk or syrup	200–300
Pitcher, water, up to 10″ height	300–400
Pitcher, water, 10″ up	400–600
Plate, up to 6″	100–150
Plate, 7″ to 9″	175–225
Plate or platter, 10″–12″	300–400
Punch bowl with base	2000–5000
Trays (oval or rectangular, also known as celery, pickle, ice cream dishes)	400–600
Tumbler, up to 12 oz.	75–125
Tumbler, over 12 oz.	100–150
Vase, up to 6″ height	100–150
Vase, 7″–10″	175–225
Vase, 11″–14″	250–350
Vase, over 14″	400–600

Czechoslovakian Glass

Czechoslovakia was officially recognized as a separate country in 1918. Before the country broke up in 1992, a good deal of glass was made by several firms. Much of it is simply marked "Czechoslovakia" or "Made in Czechoslovakia," but older items contain a wide variety of manufacturers' marks. It was made in many styles from colored Art (especially orange) to engraved crystal.

1980s Czechoslovakian Glass Advertisement

The most famous name in Czechoslovakian glass is that of Moser. The original Moser Glass Works was founded by Leo Moser in Karlsbad (presently Karlovy Vary), Czechoslovakia. Moser developed artistic forms, including orchid-colored glass named Alexandrite (separate from Webb's of England); carved animal forms, especially birds in flight and floral designs upon glass, and applied gold leaf and other enameling to glass.

Moser glass is generally priced comparably to other Art Glass forms, depending on style, work-

Moser Glass Works

manship, and overall size of the piece. Other Czechoslovakian glass is a little cheaper and is usually priced in the $50 to $100 range. These items include baskets, serving bowls, decanters, pitchers, and vases. The rarest and most elaborate designs are perfume bottles featuring amber and amethyst colors with figural stoppers (some nude). Perfume bottles have recently sold as high as $500.

Beware of cheaper Victorian figures that are similar to the older and more expensive Mary Gregory glass produced by the Boston & Sandwich Glass Company in America. The newer Czechoslovakian pieces are generally worth about a quarter to a third of the original Mary Gregory items.

Depression Glass

Depression Glass includes nearly all glass made in America from the 1920s and 1930s. Despite the fact that in the 1930s America was in its worst Depression ever, more patterns, shapes, and colors were produced in this period than in any other, past or present, in American glass history. The reason was that America's industrial revolution finally caught up with the glass industry. Glass objects were cheaply produced by machine in great quantities; before the Depression era, it was almost exclusively made by hand.

Furthermore, glass was marketed to middle- and working-class Americans, since they could now afford it. Individual pieces and large complete sets could be purchased from local general or department stores, from factory outlets, by mail order, and wherever house furnishings and kitchenware were sold. Table sets usually included

Indiana Glass Co.   Jeanette Glass Co.

Hazel Atlas Glass Co.   Hocking Glass Co.

soup and serving bowls, tumblers, plates, and saucers. Added to these could be creamers and sugars, punch sets, vases, candy and cracker jars, water pitchers, butter dishes, dessert dishes, serving platters, salt and pepper shakers, measuring cups, and nearly everything imaginable for the table. Some sets number more than one hundred distinct pieces in the same pattern!

The 1920s and '30s in America were a period of color, and glass was no exception. Colored, nonopaque glass was used as cheap prizes at fairs and exhibitions; complete sets were given away as promotional items with furniture and appliance purchases; and smaller pieces served as bonuses in oatmeal cans, cereal boxes, and household supply

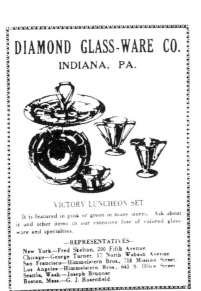

1929 Diamond Glass-Ware Advertisement

containers. Since glass was so cheap and readily available, middle- and working-class Americans purchased it in large quantities.

Pink was by far the most common color, which is evidenced by the slightly lower value of pink Depression Glass. In terms of quantity, green was a close second to pink, followed by amber. Other colors are a bit rarer (and some more valuable), such as cobalt blue, light blue, amethyst, black, yellow, ultramarine, aqua, iridescent, and ruby red.

The popularity of Depression Glass faltered in the late 1930s, as Americans tired of the colored glass. A return to crystal as well as new technological advances in ceramics and plastics ended the era of one of the most notable and prolific periods in American glass history. Depression Glass was packed away for years until collectors of the 1960s began reassembling sets. A major resurgence in Depression Glass popularity ever since has produced a multitude of collectors; skyrocketing prices; numerous clubs, books, and newsletters; and simply the most popular glass collecting medium in America.

The simple chart in this section will aid you in the quick pricing of common Depression Glass patterned items. Generally, the prices listed are for the colors pink, amber, ultramarine, iridescent, and green; increase them by 5–10 percent for green. Double the prices for amethyst, blue (cobalt or light blue), ruby red, and yellow. For the rare black, triple them. For plain crystal, reduce them by half. For plain glass without patterns, reduce the prices by 75 percent. Keep in mind that there are many rare patterns and designs that do not fall into this pricing.

Item	Price Range
Ashtray or coaster	$ 4–5
Bowls, up to 5″	8–10
Bowls, 6″–7″	10–15
Bowls, 8″–9″	20–30
Bowls, over 9″	35–50
Butter dish with cover	150–200
Cake plate with legs or feet	15–25
Candlestick	15–25
Candy jar with cover	35–50
Compote or comport, open (without cover)	20–30
Cracker jar with cover	40–60
Creamer and sugar (set)	35–50
Cruet with stopper	35–50
Cup	8–12
Decanter with stopper	100–125
Goblet	15–25
Gravy boat with platter (usually rare)	500–750
Ice bucket with tab handles	75–150
Jelly or nut dish	8–12
Ladle	15–20
Nappy (see bowls)	
Parfait	10–15
Pitcher, milk or syrup	75–100
Pitcher, water, up to 10″ height	35–50
Pitcher, water, 10″ up	50–75
Plate or saucer, up to 6″	5–7
Plate, 7″–9″	10–15
Plate or platter, 10″–12″	20–30
Punch bowl with base	250–300
Relish dish, divided	15–20
Salt and pepper shaker set	35–50
Sandwich tray with center handle	50–75
Sherbet or dessert dish	5–7
Shot glass or whiskey tumbler	7–10
Tray	25–35
Tumbler, up to 12 oz.	15–20
Tumbler, over 12 oz.	20–25
Vase, up to 8″ height	20–25
Vase, over 8″	30–50

Disney Glass

Disney glass collectibles feature Disney characters in one form or another. Decorated tumblers and glass mugs with such characters as Cinderella, Mickey Mouse, the Rescuers Down Under, Sleeping Beauty, and Winnie the Pooh sell in the $10 to $15 range. A few older ones released prior to the 1970s such as Snow White and the Seven Dwarfs, Dumbo, *Jungle Book* characters, Lady and the Tramp, and Alice in Wonderland, are selling in the $25 to $40 range.

Since the mid-1980s, Disney has been commissioning various hand-crafted crystal figurines from noted European artists. These Disney characters have been released in limited editions (usually 1,000 to 2,500 pieces) and are usually sold out very quickly. These figurines have included Dopey, Jiminy Cricket, the Little Mermaid, Mickey Mouse, Mickey Mouse as the Sorcerer's Apprentice, Tinker Bell, Winnie the Pooh, and Tigger. The figures generally retail for about $125. The Franklin Mint has also recently made available a small pewter Mickey Mouse as the Sorcerer's Apprentice riding a crystal wave; it sells for about $175.

Fenton Glass

Until the early 1930s, the Fenton Art Glass Company was primarily a Carnival Glass manufacturer. Of the big five Carnival Glass makers, Fenton is the only company to survive today. Fenton also produced a few colored patterns during the Depression era, such as Lincoln Inn.

Since the Carnival and Depression glass periods, Fenton is noted most for its fancy art baskets and its Crest designed glass. The baskets have been made in a huge variety of colors and styles, including opalescent, satin, iridescent, fancy patterned, and nearly every beautiful color

Fenton Art Glass Paper Label

that has ever been created in glass. Some baskets made less than fifty years ago, such as light blue and cranberry opalescent designs, are already selling for well over $100. Most are priced in the $30 to $75 range.

The Crest line is a large set of functional tableware and vases that includes well over a hundred pieces. Crest is basically milk glass with three separate trim designs. Aqua Crest is milk glass with a blue trim; Emerald Crest has an emerald green trim; and Silver Crest, interestingly enough, has a clear glass trim for a unique effect.

Aqua Crest was the original, dating from 1941. Silver Crest followed in 1943; it remains the most popular and is still in production today. Emerald Crest was made only in the late 1940s and 1950s and is the most valuable of the three. In dating pieces, the formula for the base milk color was changed in 1958; the originals have a very light opalescence to them when held up to a light. The Fenton signature also appears on all products made after 1973.

Generally, the larger the piece, the higher the price. Such items as plates, saucers, cups, and smaller bowls and vases sell in the $15 to $25 range. Mid-size pieces such as serving bowls, cake plates, candle holders, creamer and sugar sets, and larger vases sell in the $30 to $60 range. Large pieces such as epergnes, water pitchers, and punch bowls are priced well over $100.

Fire King Ovenware

Anchor Hocking's Fire King oven- and dinnerware includes many patterns and designs made from the late 1930s through the 1970s. A ton of it has been showing up in recent auctions, flea markets, and antique and glass shows. About the only rare and valuable items in the Fire King line are the original Hocking Philbe pattern produced in 1937–1938. These items were produced in typical Depression colors along with some platinum trimming. The saucer alone is worth about $30. The saucer is gen-

Anchor Hocking Glass Corp.

erally the least valuable piece in any table set. Rare Philbe water pitchers are worth about $1,000 while prices for covered jars (e.g., candy or cookie) have been exceeding $500.

Though it is not advisable to use the original Philbe Fire King for oven use, all Fire King made is heat-resistant for use in the oven, an advance over Depression Glass. After the Depression and the merger with Anchor, an incredible amount of Fire King products can be found in a wide variety of styles. Note that Fire King was produced before widespread household use of the microwave oven, for which its use is not recommended. There have been reports of microwaves causing cracks in some older Fire King products because of quick and sudden temperature changes.

Fire King products have been produced in many colors; most are opaque, such as jadeite (a pale lime-colored green), white, cream, ivory, gray, peach, iridescent, pink, and blue. Many of the

1937 Fire King Patent Design

lighter colors contain fired-on decals, such as flowers, birds, and wheat.

For the most part, more recent Fire King products are reasonably priced; however, assembling all of them would pose a challenge, since there are so many different patterns as well as colors. Smaller to mid-size pieces such as bowls, cups or mugs, plates, saucers, creamers, sugars, tumblers, and loaf pans sell for a few dollars. Larger pieces in the $10 to $20 range include platters, cake and baking pans, casserole dishes with covers, and pie plates.

French Art Glass

The nineteenth-century Art Glass movement in both Europe and America had its origins in France. The leader of the Art Nouveau movement in Europe, Emile Gallé was a designer and innovator, most noted for the revival of cameo engraving in multiple layers. He was careful to sign all of his creations, which inspired others to do so.

Cameo glass is made in two or more layers; the first (inner) is usually dark, and the casing (outer) is

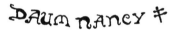

Daum Nancy Glass, France

St. Louis, France   Baccarat Glass Co.

Emile Gallé

white. Classic, floral, natural, and other scenes were carved in as many as five layers. The technique was applied by other glass artisans in England and other countries. Gallé, the Daum factory (also known as Nancy Daum or Cristalleries de Nancy), and a host of others were noted for some of the finest cameo glass ever produced. Other Art decorating techniques utilized were intaglio, inlaid, enameled, acid cutting, and copper wheel engraving.

Cameo engraved glass as well as most French Art Glass is extremely valuable and usually auctions for several hundred to several thousand dollars. Much of it can be found in the major art museums of America and Europe. Beware of "French" cameo glass produced by Romania since the 1960s, much of it signed with the older signatures.

A few other noteworthy French companies and designers include Baccarat, Lalique, Clichy, and St. Louis. Clichy and St. Louis are noted for paperweights. The original Baccarat company was most famous for high-quality millefiori and other paperweights in the mid-nineteenth century; however, it did produce a variety of other Art Glass objects. Since 1953, it has resumed paperweight production and is also noteworthy for high-quality clear lead crystal products.

René Lalique worked in the 1890s as a jeweler making paste glass jewelry.

Lalique Advertisement

LALIQUE   A.LALIQUE

M. F. Coty contracted Lalique to design perfume bottles, and Lalique's glass creations propelled him into a position as France's premier designer of the twentieth century. Lalique's figure glass is usually made of quality lead crystal and may be frosted or enameled; a few rare items were produced in black. The figures are often formed into useful objects and may be molded or blown in several identical views. Figures also may be cameo-engraved or heavily etched and contain smooth, satiny acidized or pearlized finishes.

Dating is a big problem with Lalique glass. Older molds have been reused, but some signed marks are helpful. Up to his death in 1945, most were marked "R. Lalique." The "R" was dropped a little later. Other pieces may contain "R. Lalique, France" for a signature.

Heisey Glass

The A. H. Heisey Glass Company had its origins in Newark, Ohio, in the 1860s. Early on, Heisey was noted for cut patterns and finely etched glass. Like many others in the late nineteenth and early twentieth centuries, Heisey experimented with colors and decorating techniques and produced some Art Glass items in opalescent, milk, custard, vaseline, alexandrite, and some silver/platinum trim. It also produced a few iridescent Carnival Glass wares.

As far as collectibles are concerned, the famous Heisey crystal animals produced from the

1920s Heisey Glass Advertisement

A. H. Heisey Glass Co.

1920s until the factory closed in 1957 are the most collectible. Nearly all exceed $100 when auctioned or sold, and a few rare ones, such as the frosted tropical fish, are approaching $1,000. Be sure to examine animals closely before buying; the originals were sold as toys and many are scratched and damaged from rough play by children! Heisey's cut glass, pressed wares, Carnival Glass, Art items, and other glass products are comparably priced to those of other producers in the same category.

Hobnail Glass

Hobnail is a very popular cut or pressed pattern that resembles small raised knobs referred to as "hobs" or "prunts." The name originated in England from the large heads of hobnail fasteners. Hobnail glass is one of those rare patterns that has been available in nearly every significant glass movement over the past two centuries. It has been

1926 Westmoreland Advertisement

cut, pressed, decorated, and colored in most Art forms, and made into both Carnival and Depression glass. Most rare Carnival hobnail pieces produced by the Millersburg Glass Company are worth several hundred dollars.

Westmoreland began making a pattern called English Hobnail in the 1920s in typical Depression colors. The pattern was popular and continued as one of Westmoreland's steady sellers into the 1970s. Since a significant quantity was produced, the majority of Westmoreland's hobnail glassware is reasonably priced, in the $15 to $50 range. A few minor pieces such as plates and saucers are under $10, while a few harder-to-find pieces such as decanters, water pitchers, and vases exceed $100.

Irish Glass

Glass has been made in Ireland for centuries, and much of it was and still is exported to the United States. The most famous name is Waterford, which contains a separate listing in this chapter. Aside from the city of Waterford, the towns of Cork and Dublin also house large factories and produced significant quantities of glass in the past. Over the past two decades, many small Irish manufacturers have been established which have been producing collectible glass. The Kerry Glass name can be found on glass animals and paperweights, made with forty varying shades of swirled green colors. The paperweights retail in the $25 to $40 range. Tipperary produces crystal stemware, tableware, vases, and a few novelty items such as miniature glass slippers and footballs. Galway is another Irish company, which produces tableware, covered jars, and miniatures such as little cut crystal grandfather clocks. The clocks retail in the $75 to $100 range.

Kitchen Glassware

Kitchen glassware became very popular during the Depression era and includes a wide variety of items—so many in fact, that a chart is necessary. The basic colors include pink, green, amber, yel-

1928 Butler Brothers Catalogue Insert

low, and light blue. For opaque versions and crystal, reduce the prices given by 50 percent. For cobalt blue, ruby red, or ultramarine, double the prices. For black, quadruple the prices. As with all pricing, keep in mind that there are many rare patterns and designs that do not fall into this pricing.

ITEM	PRICE RANGE
Bowls, mixing	10–20
Butter dish with cover	25–50
Canisters with cover	25–50
Cruet with stopper	15–25
Egg cup	25–35
Juice dispenser	75–100
Knife	25–50
Ladle	15–20
Measuring cup	15–25
Pie dish	35–50
Syrup pitcher	50–75
Reamer	10–20
Refrigerator dish with cover	15–50
Rolling pin	100–125

Kitchenware can be difficult to identify at times because of the many plain and unmarked styles. These products were made in every color, including the opaque styles of delphite blue, jadeite green, custard yellow or beige, milk whites, and fired-on colors. Many were decorated by embossing and enameling as well as the widespread use of fired-on decals or transfers. Beware of damage from heavy use.

Some of the largest makers of kitchen products during the Depression era were Hocking/Anchor Hocking (many canister sets, Vitrock, Fire King, and nearly every type of piece made); Jeannette (Jennyware products—most made in ultramarine and some in other colors); Hazel Atlas (famous for the Crisscross pattern); and McKee (many opaque and milk-white patterns—some with colored dots, red or black ships, etc.); but there are a host of others.

Lamps/Lighting

The most significant object produced during the late-nineteenth century Art Nouveau period in America was the Tiffany lamp. The world-renowned Tiffany lamps are now commanding auction prices in excess of $100,000 for many of the larger works. Reproductions pose some problems, and you should watch for fraudulent copies. A vast majority of the original lamps are signed "L.C.T.," "Louis C. Tiffany," "Tiffany Studios," or other titles containing the word "Tiffany."

Tiffany was not the only producer of high-quality glass lamps but is, rather, credited with spawning the movement. Some of the most exquisite lamps ever made in America were fabricated by Handel and signed by numerous individual artists working for the company. Prices for Handel lamps as well as lamps made by other Art Glass companies rival those for Tiffany.

Art Glass lamps contain a wide variety of styles

and experimental designs. Chipped glass effects, hand-decorated interiors, bent inserts, metal or leaded shades, fired-on metallic stains, gilding, cameo engraving, and etchings can all be found

Handel and Co.

on lamps. Even the bases were typically quite elaborate; copper, brass, bronze, and white plated metals were used and decorated as well. Today, small lamps are still made in the Tiffany style and retail for several hundred dollars.

Libbey Glass

Libbey had its origins as the New England Glass Company in 1818. The name was changed in the 1870s when the company was purchased by William L. Libbey. The New England Glass Company was founded by Deming Jarves, an early pioneer who was very instrumental in getting glassmaking started in America. New England Glass was blessed with many other gifted designers—Joseph Locke, Henry Whitney, and Louis Vaupel, to name just a few.

The company's output was huge and spanned all lines of glass from early pressed practical wares to fancy Art Glass. New England's Art examples

W. L. Libbey & Son

included Agata, Amberina, and Pomona, among a host of others. The lines were continued by Libbey until they went out of fashion. Libbey was also a very significant cut glass producer, so significant that it is known as the largest producer of cut glass in the world. Its products rivaled the best anywhere and have won numerous awards at various expositions.

Libbey was not known to make Carnival Glass or much in the way of Depression Glass patterns; however, it did produce a lot of plain practical glassware, such as tumblers, that was sold in great quantities to hotels and restaurants. Combined with New England, Libbey is the oldest and one of the largest producers of glass products today.

Marbles

The Akro Agata Company is responsible for much of America's early marble production. It began as a marble manufacturer in 1914 and quickly became America's leading maker of marbles. Its marbles were made in solid, opaque, transparent, and swirled colors. Its most famous and collectible designs included the onyx spiraled colors of red, blue, yellow, green, etc.

Look for Agata products in the original boxes. Marbles were typically packaged in 5-, 10-, 25-, 50-, and 100-piece boxes and generally sell for about $1.00 to $1.50 per marble. Other products include a 36-piece Chinese Checker set, which is worth about $75.

In the 1930s, several manufacturers expanded into marble production, which forced Agata to manufacture other products, such as novelty items. A few novelty manufacturers today continue to

Akro Agate Co.

produce high-quality swirled glass marbles. The Gibson Glass Company, for instance, produces some large fancy handmade marbles that retail in the $10 to $20 range.

Milk Glass

Milk glass is opaque glassware that derives its white color from the addition of calcined bones or tin to the formula. It was most popular during the late nineteenth century in America and served as a cheaper substitute to more expensive European glass and porcelain products. Milk glass was shaped into most tableware items; however, the most popular products are covered animal dishes such as roosters, hens, sheep, dogs, squirrels, rabbits, deer, turkeys, ducks, and other birds (swans and songbirds). Usually, the bottom dish is an oval or round base while the animal makes up the cover. Original dishes generally sell in the $75 to $150 range.

A problem is identifying what is original and what is newer. The most prevalent original manufacturers included McKee, Challinor-Taylor, Flaccus, and Atterbury. The age of McKee pieces is particularly difficult to determine because some original covers were not marked. A lot of milk glass covered dishes were made throughout the twentieth century, and most are not marked as well.

One of the largest milk glass table sets ever made was Westmoreland's Panel Grape pattern in the 1950s through the 1970s. Some pieces (mostly plates) are also available with birds, flowers, and fruits for color decoration applied on the white. Lesser pieces sell in the $15 to $25 range and include plates, bowls, cups, candle holders, and goblets. Larger pieces such as covered candy and butter dishes, pitchers, vases, and trays sell in the $30 to $50 range. Even though Panel Grape is a fairly recent pattern, there are already many rare pieces that exceed $100 in value. These include a candelabrum, covered canisters, condiment and dresser sets, epergnes, large circular platters, and punch bowls.

Miniatures

Cut or faceted crystal miniatures have been around for only the past two decades or so and are already highly collectible. They are primarily made in European countries, including Austria, Germany, Sweden, and France, but a few are made in the United States. They are found mostly in jewelry and gift stores. Most are faceted and animals are the most popular medium, though new unique and larger items are appearing constantly. Colors are primarily used for accents, though some pieces contain more surface area of color than crystal.

The pricing for miniatures is almost solely based on the relative size of the piece in question. Tiny faceted animals such as bears, rabbits, cats, dogs, mice and birds that are less than inch in height or an inch long sell in the $15 to $30 range. Those in the one-inch to two-inch range sell for $30 to $50. Larger animals and other crystal items such as airplanes, castles, trains, lighthouses, mansions, carousels, and slot machines often exceed $100. There are even a few pieces that exceed $1,000, such as a giant eight-inch turtle and a four-inch square replica of the Taj Mahal.

Mount Washington/Pairpoint

The original Mount Washington Glass Company was founded by Deming Jarves for his son George in 1837. In the 1860s and 1870s, the company changed hands several times, and it was once controlled by the Libbey family. Mount Washington was a major producer of Art Glass tableware and vases in the late nineteenth century. A huge variety

Crown Milano

Pairpoint Mfg. Co./ Mt. Washington Glass Works

"Crown Milano" Mt. Washington Glass Works

"Royal Flemish" Mt. Washington Glass Works

Mt. Washington Glass Works Paper Labels

Pairpoint Mfg. Co.

of styles and designs, including albertine, Amberina, Burmese, cameo-engraved, Crown Milano, mother-of-pearl, lava glass, Peach Blow, and countless others were all part of the company's output. One of its own patents was Royal Flemish glassware, which resembles stained windows (individual pieces of glass separated by lead line borders).

Pairpoint merged with Mount Washington in 1894 and eventually assumed all its glass manufacturing operations. Pairpoint produced a wide variety of items from functional tableware and lamps to fancy Art Glass and cut designs. Robert Gunderson and Robert Bryden were also active with the firm in the mid-twentieth century.

Because of their age, Mount Washington products are more valuable than the newer Pairpoint.

1880s Mt. Washington Advertisement

Simple Art items produced by Mount Washington such as bowls, candlesticks, plates, and shakers typically sell in the $100 to $300 range. Large elaborate items can easily reach several thousand dollars; they include cameo-engraved pieces, lamps, water pitchers, and various Art Glass vases. Most Pairpoint pieces are in the $100 to $300 range.

Opalescent Glass

Opalescence consists of a milky or cloudy coloring or coating on glass. The base glass is usually colored in bluish-green or ultramarine, although other colors, including crystal, are fairly common as well. A heavier milk color usually appears at the top of opalescent pieces. The coloring is achieved by adding tin, zinc, and ash from bone to a hot piece of glass and then refiring the object.

Opalescent glass can be found in blown objects, pressed items, and novelties such as corncob vases. The crown jewels as well as the most valuable pieces are those created in cranberry opalescence. Older cranberry opalescent pieces from the late nineteenth and early twentieth centuries, such as vases, cruets with stoppers, baskets, coin dot patterns, bubble lattice designs (vases and pitchers), and other Art-related items easily sell for several hundred dollars. Newer items and older pressed items are still fairly reasonably priced in the $50 to $100 range.

Paperweights

Paperweights are a broad category with origins as far back as ancient Egypt. In modern times, a major movement known as the classical period of paper-weights occurred in France in the 1840s and 1850s. The three primary manufacturers were Baccarat, Clichy, and St. Louis. The big three were responsi-ble for creating the finest examples of Art Glass paperweights. Originals are worth several hundred to several thousand dollars. Other quality makers of this era included English, Bohemian, and Venetian glass artisans.

Paperweight production carried over to America to such early companies as New England and Boston & Sandwich, but the fad quickly phased out in the later nineteenth century. The popularity of paperweights resurfaced in the mid-twentieth cen-tury, and a wide variety of new artists and new com-panies such as Correia and Perthshire produce paperweights in quantity as well as limited produc-tion items.

Peach Blow Art Glass

The key coloring agent in Peach Blow is produced by adding cobalt or copper oxide in the general for-mula. The shading of Peach Blow varies from a light grayish-blue color at the base to a rose pink or peach color at the top. Cobalt generally produces a slightly darker shade at the base than copper.

Peach Blow can be found in numerous finishes, patterns, and enamels. It tends to be thin and fragile and is desirable and valuable. Peach Blow was produced by several companies, such as Mount Washington/Pairpoint; Hobbs, Brocunier; New Martinsville; New England/Libbey; and the English company of Thomas Webb & Sons.

Peach Blow items are gener-ally rarer and more valuable than most Art Glass styles. A few smaller items such as bowls, candlesticks, tumblers, and

Photo by Robin Rainwater

Peach Blow Art Glass

plates can be found in the $100 to $200 range; how-ever, the vast majority of pieces sell for several hun-dred to several thousand dollars. Large serving bowls, cruets with stoppers, pitchers, and large vases usually exceed $1,000 at auctions and antique stores.

Pressed Glass

Pressed patterns are some of the oldest styles of collectible glass that were made in some quantity. They are for the most part nineteenth-century hand-pressed items that vary a good deal in consis-tency. Further complicating matters is the general lack of patents, and hence numerous companies and individuals making the same designs in different molds. The end result is objects with wide varia-tions in shape, pattern, type, and general formula. Ribbing may be thicker or thinner; vines may be single or double; gridding or checkering maybe be narrow or wide; and even clear glass tends to tinge a pale purple with age. Manganese in the basic for-mula is responsible for amethyst coloring; a little too much coupled with prolonged exposure to the sun is responsible for this tinting.

Beware of tinging as well as serious flaws within old pattern glass. Some clear Depression patterns and reproductions can be confused with older and more valuable pressed glass designs. Thinner exam-ples can be quite fragile, but for the most part the

PRESCUT

McKee-Jeannette Glass Works

McKee Glass Co.

Hobbs, Brocunier & Co.

H. C. Fry Glass Co.

"Iris" Fostoria Glass Co.
Paper Label

Imperial Glass Co.

formulas used in pressed glass have held together well. Look out for irregular, out-of-balance, or slightly stretched pieces, or ones that appear off-center, including the pattern.

Here is a simple chart for the quick pricing of common pressed glass patterned items. Common patterns include circles, diamonds, facets, hobnails or beads, panels, ribs, columns, ropes, shells, scales, vines, stars, squares, rectangles, swirls, and bull's-eyes Generally, the prices listed are for clear glass. For common colors such as green,

1901 U.S. Glass Catalogue Insert

amber, yellow, ultramarine, light blue, and frosted designs, increase them by 50 percent. Double the prices for cobalt blue and ruby red. For a few fancy Art colors, such as cranberry and chocolate, quadruple the prices. Keep in mind that there are many rare patterns and designs that do not fall into this pricing.

ITEM	PRICE RANGE
Ashtray or Coaster	$ 5–10
Bowls, up to 5″	15–20
Bowls, 6″–7″	20–30
Bowls, 8″–9″	30–40
Bowls, over 9″	50–75
Butter dish with cover	75–100
Cake plate with legs or feet	50–75
Candlestick	15–25
Candy jar with cover	50–75
Celery vase	40–75
Compote or comport, open (without cover)	40–60
Cordial	25–50
Creamer and sugar (set)	75–100
Cruet with stopper	50–75
Cup	10–20
Decanter with stopper	75–125
Goblet	25–50
Jam jar with lid	30–50
Pitcher, milk or syrup	50–75
Pitcher, water, up to 10″ height	50–75
Pitcher, water, 10″ up	75–100
Plate or saucer, up to 6″	10–15
Plate, 7″–9″	15–20
Plate or Platter, 10″–12″	50–100
Relish dish, divided	15–25
Salt and pepper shaker set	30–50
Sauce dish	10–20
Spooner or spoon holder	15–25
Shot glass or whiskey tumbler	10–15
Sugar shaker	25–50
Tray	50–100
Tumbler, up to 12 oz.	15–25
Tumbler, over 12 oz.	25–35
Vase, up to 8″ height	25–40
Vase, over 8″	40–60

Ruby Red Glass

If you have been reading closely to this point, you have probably noticed the little pricing notes concerning ruby red glass. Most say to double the value of the piece if it has been produced in full or solid ruby red. A good deal of the value comes from the metallic gold coloring agent necessary to produce the deep rich red color.

Ruby red was also used as a stain in glassware produced in the late nineteenth and early twentieth centuries. The stain was applied to clear pressed glass and often shows up on souvenir glass etched with the name of a fair, exposition, city, or even a person's name. Common items include toy mugs, shot glasses, toothpick holders, vases, and common tableware such as bowls, plates, trays, goblets, pitchers, and tumblers. Smaller stained items are usually priced in the $20 to $50 range, while large items are generally in the $50 to $100 range. A few odd items such as coin dot Art designs, fancy covered jars, and other art patterns exceed $100.

Beware of reproduction pieces with ruby staining. For the most part, the newer stains are much weaker in color than the originals. Beginning in 1938, Anchor Hocking produced a set of tableware called Royal Ruby that is usually considered as later than the Depression era. The pattern is named for the color, which is a little darker than ordinary ruby red. Anchor Hocking has a patent on the Royal Ruby name. Both Royal Ruby and its sister pattern, Forest Green (a caliginous emerald green that is darker than ordinary Depression green) were made

Ruby Overlay Glass

Photo by Robin Rainwater

in great quantities, and pieces are usually not too difficult to find. Prices for all pieces in Royal Ruby and Forest Green are inexpensive and generally sell in the $5 to $40 range—much cheaper than original ruby or ruby-stained items.

Shot Glasses

Shot glasses are small glass articles that generally hold an ounce or two of liquid and are three inches in height or less. Shot glasses have been around since the 1830s and cover just about every category of glass. The most desirable by collectors are the pre-Prohibition-era whiskey sample or advertising glasses. Most contain etched white writing of a distiller, company, proprietor, or other alcohol-related advertising. These glasses sell for around $20 to $40, but recently some rare examples have auctioned off in excess of $100. Shot glass collectors are usually quantity collectors often boasting hundreds and even a thousand or two glasses! Below is listed some basic pricing guidelines for shot glasses:

BASIC PRICING CATEGORY	PRICE RANGE
Plain shot glasses with or without flutes	50¢–75¢
General with an enameled design	$ 2–3
General advertising	3–4
Whiskey or beer advertising—Modern	4–5
Pop or soda advertising (e.g., Coke or Pepsi)	12–15
General etched designs	5–7
General with gold designs	6–8
General frosted designs	3–4
Frosted with gold designs	6–8
Culver 22-karat gold	5–7
General porcelain	4–6
Black porcelain replica	3–4
Standard glasses with pewter	7–10
Square shot glasses–general	5– 7
Square glasses with etching	7–10
Square glasses with pewter	12–15
Square glasses with two-tone bronze/pewter	15–17
Taiwan tourist	1–2
General tourist	2–3

Porcelain tourist	3–4
Turquoise and gold tourist	5–7
Depression tall tourist	5–7
Depression colors	7–10
Depression colors—patterns or etching	15–25
Depression tall—general designs	6–8
Carnival colors—plain or fluted	35–45
Carnival colors with patterns	50–60
Rounded European designs with gold rims	4–5
Glasses with inside eyes	5–7
Nude shot glasses	20–25
Barrel-shaped	5–7
Mary Gregory/Anchor Hocking ships	100–150
Tiffany/Gallé/fancy Art	500–750
Nineteenth-century cut patterns	25–35
Ruby flashed glasses	30–40
Whiskey sample glasses	25–50

Photo by Robin Rainwater

Pressed, Fostoria Whirlpool, and Cut Star

Souvenir Glass

Some of the earliest glass souvenirs were made in 1876 for the nation's Centennial celebration; the most popular were glass Liberty Bells. Original mold-embossed Liberty Bells stamped with "1876" are now selling for a little over $100. Except for fancy Art Glass or colors such as ruby red and custard, the price of souvenir glass varies with age; the older the item, the higher its value.

In the 1880s into the Depression years, ruby flashed or ruby stained items were quite popular and appeared in small tumblers, toothpick holders, toy mugs, goblets, vases, and some tableware (see

Photo by Robin Rainwater

Souvenir Ruby Red Tumbler

"Ruby Red Glass" for pricing information). Custard glass, which is a yellowish-cream colored opaque glass, was also a popular medium for souvenir items. The prices for custard items rival those of ruby red.

Today, souvenirs abound with fired-on decals or machine-applied enamels; these include tumblers, mugs, shot glasses, and a wide variety of other items. Modern souvenir glass articles sell for as little as $1 or $2 up to about $10.

Steuben Glass

Steuben was founded by Frederick Carder and Thomas J. Hawkes. Hawkes was a maker of superb quality crystal, while Carder, like Tiffany, studied the Art movement in Europe as well as various Art styles from around the world. Carder became a world-class designer and the majority of Steuben's Art colored art creations are attributed to him or at the very least under his direction. The majority of the objects created were signed "Steuben" or with Carder's signature.

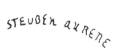

Steuben Glass Works

Steuben Glass Works

"Cire Perdue" Steuben
Glass Works

In general, Steuben Art products are priced similarly to other high-quality art glass. Lesser pieces may sell for $150 to $250 (e.g., bowls, plates, and small vases) while larger and more unique Art styles may reach into the thousands. One of those unique styles that was exclusively Steuben's was Aurene.

Aurene is Steuben's most noteworthy and valuable Art Glass design. It was produced in five basic colors: blue, brown, gold, green, and red. It remains as Steuben's most desirable and popular colored glass designs; however, it is quite scarce today. Aurene is characterized by an iridescent sheen applied by spraying on various metallic salts and other chemical mixtures. Base colors were ordinarily clear, amber, or topaz. Matte finishes were applied by spraying on tin or iron chloride solutions. Alabaster and calcite were necessary for the green and red colors.

From 1933 on, Steuben concentrated almost exclusively on production of the highest grade of crystal. A few deviations such as silver or gold accents have been added, but no complete colored

Various Frederick Carder Signatures, Steuben Glass Works

Photo by Robin Rainwater

Steuben Vase

pieces have been produced since. Steuben's grade of crystal rivals any made in the world today. All modern crystal items contain the "Steuben" signature in fine diamond point script. The least inexpensive modern Steuben items are hollow Christmas ornaments that sell for $95. Hand coolers in the shape of small animals sell for $150. Generally, the larger the piece, the higher the price. A few limited-edition major works (hand-engraved sculptured glass), such as Moby Dick, gazelle and swan bowls, and Grecian urns, sell in the $25,000 to $50,000 range.

Thimbles

Glass thimbles are fairly new to the collector world. Glass thimbles are made in both America and Europe, most over the past two decades. A standard-size thimble is about an inch in height, though many glass thimbles are taller because of a decorative finial on top.

Ruffled or spun crystal thimbles including finials usually sell in the $8 to $10 range. Cut glass patterned and engraved thimbles that may be in crystal and colors or a combination of the two sell in the $15 to $25 range. The most expensive glass thimbles are those produced in cobalt blue or ruby red with a miniature paperweight design in the top. Paperweight thimbles sell for $35 to $40.

Tiffany Art Glass

Louis Comfort Tiffany was an American painter as well as the son of the jewelry magnate who had founded Tiffany & Co., the famous jewelry store.

Louis C. Tiffany

Furnaces Inc. Favrile

"Favrile" Tiffany

His painting career did not blossom, and he decided to explore unique forms in art glass. The change was a positive one and soon earned him a reputation as the American leader of the Art Nouveau period. He opened a small glass factory in 1878 and experimented with stained glass color effects. Glass windows were produced without using stains or paints but, rather, with colored glass fragments. The color, detail, and illusion were created within the glass itself by plating one layer of glass over another.

Tiffany broadened his work to include lamps and was one of the first to experiment with iridescent glass. He named his iridescent products Favrile or Tiffany Favrile. Favrile was unique in that all ornamentation was completed within the glass and excluded all external decoration. Tiffany began as an individual artist. To study the Art trends in Europe, Tiffany visited Paris in 1889 and observed Gallé's work in person at the Exposition Universelle. In 1896, Tiffany began commercial production, and the Tiffany factory produced thousands of items into the early 1930s.

Along with unique color effects and experimentation with iridescent forms, Tiffany products can be found with enamels and expensive metallic designs (bronze, gold, silver, platinum, etc.). Tiffany's factory also produced items solely in metal and pottery. Most Tiffany products are signed in one form or another, such as "L.C.T.," "L. C. Tiffany," "Tiffany Studios," "Louis C. Tiffany Furnaces," or "Favrile Tiffany."

Original Tiffany Art products along with their prices are at the height of the Art Glass world. It is difficult to find Tiffany products for $500; occasionally, a small vase, plate, stamp box, or small bowl in a common art pattern may be found for less than this amount. Larger and more unique Art styles like Favrile easily reach into the thousands. Favrile was originally developed and patented in 1892. It is characterized by multicolored iridescent base colors decorated with applied or embedded designs and remains as Tiffany's most famous and sought after style.

Venetian Glass

Glassmaking in Venice, especially on the island of Murano, has a long and rich history. Venetians were the first to develop a colorless glass formula in the sixteenth century, which they named cristallo. Cristallo was quickly adapted to mirrors, tableware, and objets d'art. Cristallo was eventually replaced by a more durable and workable lead glass formula discovered by George Ravenscroft in England in 1676.

Original Venetian items rarely surface, since most are in museums; however, over the past two centuries, glass production in Venice has rarely wavered. Venetian Glass is still made today on the island of Murano near Venice, utilizing many of the same designs and techniques employed for centuries. Venini is one such maker, and these items are usually signed "Venini" or "Venini Murano" or even "Murano Made in Italy." Newer Venetian items are thicker than the thin cristallo of old.

During the Art Nouveau period, Venetians were particularly noted for producing millefiore designs in paperweights and other objects. Venetian Art Glass is priced similarly to other Art items. Smaller items such as bowls, candlesticks, tumblers, and plates can be found in the $75 to $150 range, while large serving bowls, decanters with stoppers, pitchers, vases, and novelty items sell in the $150 to $500 range.

Waterford Glass

Original Waterford glass was produced between 1783 and 1851 in Waterford, Ireland. The original items were made in a fine grade of crystal that was decorated by cutting. A new factory was built in 1951, and by the 1970s Waterford has become one of the largest makers of crystal in the world.

The new Waterford is not unlike the old in

1980's–1990's Waterford Advertisement

style, that is, the production of fine crystal with cut decorations. The new items include functional tableware and stemware, clocks, chandeliers, and novelty items, all made of quality lead crystal. Many are already becoming quite collectible, too.

Typical Waterford products—goblets, bells, bowls, candle holders, clocks, plates, tumblers, and small novelty items—sell in the $50 to $100 range. Larger pieces such as cut crystal decanters, centerpieces, lamps, vases, and pitchers sell for $100 to $300. Of particular note are chandeliers and the recently handmade limited edition masterpiece

Waterford Glass

collection items. An elaborate Waterford chandelier is priced at $2,000 to $3,000, while the masterpiece items approach $1,000.

Westmoreland Glass

The company was originally established as the
Westmoreland Specialty Company in 1890. The
company processed condiments to fill its own glass
containers, and soon expanded into colored glass
tableware. Although Westmoreland produced
some rare Carnival Glass along with some Depression Glass, it is noted
most for milk glass pro-
duction and their Eng-
lish Hobnail pattern.
Westmoreland's English
Hobnail pattern was cre-
ated in the 1920s in typical Depression colors.
The pattern was popular
and continued as one of
Westmoreland's steady
sellers into the 1970s.
Since a significant quan-
tity was produced, the majority of Westmoreland's
hobnail glassware is reasonably priced, in the $15 to
$50 range. A few minor pieces such as plates and
saucers are under $10, while a few harder-to-find
pieces such as decanters, water pitchers, and vases
exceed $100.

Westmoreland Glass Co.

One of the largest milk glass table sets ever made
was Westmoreland's Panel Grape pattern in the
1950s through the 1970s. Some pieces (mostly
plates) are also available with birds, flowers, and
fruits for color decoration applied on the white.
Lesser pieces sell in the $15 to $25 range and
include plates, bowls, cups, candle holders, and
goblets. Larger pieces such as covered candy and
butter dishes, pitchers, vases, and trays sell in the
$30 to $50 range. Even though Panel Grape is a
fairly recent pattern, there are already many rare
pieces that exceed $100. These include a cande-

labrum, covered canisters, condiment and dresser sets, epergnes, large circular platters, and punch bowls.

Beware of reproductions with Westmoreland products, especially with Carnival glass. True Westmoreland Carnival Glass exceeds $1,000 in price. Original Westmoreland trademarks include a capital "W" within what appears to be an upside-down lampshade. The intertwined "W" and "G" mark was not developed until 1949. Finally, in 1983, the full name of "Westmoreland" appears as a trademark. Westmoreland closed for good in early 1985.

Whimsical Glass

As the name implies, whimsical glass items are objects created at the whim of glass workers. Many are unique and one-of-a-kind novelty items such as walking canes, miniature hat vases, marbles, candy, paperweights, witch balls, pipes, and chess sets. Miniature hat vases are found in many colors and cost as little as $5 to $10 for newer reproductions, while originals can approach $50. Witch balls are crystal balls that also come in several colors, though crystal is the most common. Originals can sell for several hundred dollars. Glass candies are made in Venice today and sell for a few dollars for one. Be careful with swirled glass candies, especially if several are together in one dish. They look so much like hard candy in twirled wrappers that you may mistake them for the real thing!

The most popular whimsical items are probably glass walking or novelty canes that range from a few inches to several feet in length. Canes are either hollow or solid and typically contain a bulb or fancy-shaped handle along with a candy-stripe color pattern, although solids are common, too. A typical cane sells for around $100, though larger, hand-blown, and fancy colors like cranberry sell for more.

CHAPTER 4

THE GLASS COLLECTOR'S RESOURCE GUIDE

GLASS MUSEUMS

Glass museums vary widely in what they have to offer. Some hold extensive collections from several different periods and categories, while others are very specific. The Corning Museum of Glass in New York State is the largest museum dedicated to glass. In addition to glassware, the facilities also include the Steuben Glass Factory and the most extensive library in the world on glassware. As part of the museum admission, the Steuben glass factory is open for public viewing.

At Corning, you will find a large collection of Art Glass, pressed glass, cut glass, and unique one-of-a-kind glass sculptures. What you will not find is much in the way of Carnival, Depression, and more modern forms of collectible glass. The Chrysler Museum in Norfolk, Virginia, is probably second to Corning in terms of how extensive and broad the collection of glass is, but it, too, lacks much in the way of twentieth-century collectible glass.

The vast majority of museums that feature glass are either very specific in their offerings or include glass with other artifacts. Many large museums in the country, such as the Art Institute of Chicago, the New York Metropolitan Museum, and the Smithsonian Institution display glass as part of other period collections. Smaller museums, such as the Cambridge Glass Museum, feature glass products manufactured by the Cambridge Glass Company.

For paperweights and other novelty items made by Degenhart, visit the Degenhart Paperweight and Glass Museum in Cambridge, Ohio. See the Fenton Art Glass Company and Museum in Williamstown, West Virginia, for an extensive collection of carnival glass. For Heisey glassware, visit the National Heisey Glass Museum in Newark, Ohio. For pressed glass made in the New England area, see the Sandwich Glass Museum in Sandwich, Massachusetts. The Toledo Museum of Art was actually founded by Libbey to hold and display much of its exhibition and one-of-a-kind glassware. This museum features an extensive cut glass collection.

About the only glass-related items that you will not find in any quantity are more modern twentieth-century forms such as Depression Glass. Some museums may have a few pieces, but until some significant donations are made, Depression Glass will remain in the hands of dealers and collectors. As it gets older, watch for Depression Glass displays to pop up all over!

Allen Art Museum
Oberlin College
Oberlin, OH 44074

Art Institute of Chicago
Michigan Ave. & Adams St.
Chicago, IL 60603

The Bennington Museum
W. Main St.
Bennington, VT 05201

Bergstrom Art Center and Museum
165 N. Park Ave.
Neenah, WI 54956

Cambridge Glass Museum
506 S. 9th St.
Cambridge, OH 43725

Carnegie Institute Museum of Art
4400 Forbes Ave.
Pittsburgh, PA 15213

Chrysler Museum at Norfolk
Olney Rd. & Mowbray Arch
Norfolk, VA 23510

Corning Museum of Glass and Glass Center
One Museum Way
Corning, NY 14830

Currier Gallery of Art
192 Orange St.
Manchester, NH 03104

Degenhart Paperweight and Glass Museum, Inc.
P.O. Box 186
Cambridge, OH 43725

Fenton Art Glass Co.
700-T Elizabeth St.
Williamstown, WV 26187

Greentown Glass Museum, Inc.
624 W. Main St.
Greentown, IN 46936

Henry Ford Museum
P.O. Box 1970
Dearborn, MI 48121

Lightner Museum
75 King St.
St. Augustine, FL 32084

Metropolitan Museum of Art
1000 Fifth Ave.
New York, NY 10028

Minneapolis Institute of Arts
2400 Third Ave. S.
Minneapolis, MN 55404

Milan Historical Museum
10 Edison Dr.
Milan, OH 44846

Museum of Beverage Containers and Advertising
1055 Ridgecrest Dr.
Goodlettsville, TN 37072

Museum of Modern Art
11 West 53rd St.
New York, NY 10019

National Bottle Museum
76 Milton Avenue
Ballston Spa, NY 12020

National Heisey Glass Museum
1609 West Church St.
Newark, OH 43055

Oglebay Institute-Mansion Museum
Oglebay Park
Wheeling, WV 26003

Old Sturbridge Village
1 Old Sturbridge Village Rd.
Sturbridge, MA 01566

Philadelphia Museum of Art
P.O. Box 7646
Philadelphia, PA 19101

Portland Art Museum
Seven Congress Square
Portland, ME 04101

Sandwich Glass Museum
P.O. Box 103
Sandwich, MA 02563

Seneca County Museum
28 Clay St.
Tiffin, OH 44883

Smithsonian Museum of History
Smithsonian Institution
Washington, DC 29560

Wadsworth Athenum
600 Main St.
Hartford, CT 06103

Toledo Museum of Art
P.O. Box 1013
Toledo, OH 43697

PERIODICALS, CLUBS, NEWSLETTERS, AND OTHER RESOURCES

Because the categories of collectible glass are so broad, there is a wide variety of periodicals, newsletters, and clubs available. Listed below are the organizations currently operating. To receive information about them, simply write to the appropriate address.

Aladdin Knights
C/O J. W. Courter
Route 1
Simpson, IL 62985

American Carnival Glass Assoc.
P.O. Box 235
Littlestown, PA 17340

American Cut Glass Assoc.
3228 S. Boulevard Ste. 221
P.O. Box 1775
Edmond, OK 73083-1775

Antique & Art Glass Salt Shaker Collectors Society
2832 Rapidan Trail
Maitland, FL 32751

The Antique Press
12403 N. Florida Ave.
Tampa, FL 33612

Antique Review
P.O. Box 538
Worthington, OH 43085-9928

The Antiques Trader
P.O. Box 1050
Dubuque, IA 52004-1050

Antique Week
27 N. Jefferson
P.O. Box 90
Knightstown, IN 46148

Arts and Crafts Quarterly
P.O. Box 3592, Station E
Trenton, NJ 08629

Avon Times
P.O. Box 9868 Dept. P
Kansas City, MO 64134

Boyd Art Glass Collectors Guild
P.O. Box 52
Hatboro, PA 19040

Cambridge Collectors Inc.
P.O. Box 416
Cambridge, OH 43725

Candlewick Club
C/O Virginia R. Scott
275 Milledge Terrace
Athens, GA 30606

**Collectible Carnival
Glass Assoc.**
C/O Wilma Thurston
2360 N. Old S.R.9
Columbus, IN 47203

**Collectors of Findlay
Glass**
P.O. Box 256
Findlay, OH 45839-0256

**Czechoslovakian
Collectors Guild
International**
P.O. Box 901395
Kansas City, MO 64190

Depression Glass Daze
P.O. Box 57
Otisville, MI 48463

**Early American Pattern
Glass Society**
P.O. Box 340023
Columbus, OH 43234

**Fenton Art Glass Col-
lectors of America, Inc.**
P.O. Box 384
Williamstown, WV
26187

**The Fostoria Glass
Society of America, Inc.**
P.O. Box 826
Moundsville, WV 26041

**Fostoria OH Glass
Assoc.**
109 North Main St.
Fostoria, OH 44830

Fruit Jar Newsletter
364 Gregory Ave.
West Orange, NJ
07052-3743

H. C. Fry Glass Society
P.O. Box 41
Beaver, PA 15009

The Glass Art Society
C/O Tom McGlauchlin
Toledo Museum of Art
Toledo, OH 43609

**Glass Collectors Club
of Toledo**
2727 Middlesex Dr.
Toledo, OH 43606

Glass Collector's Digest
P.O. Box 553
Marietta, OH 45750-
9979

**Glass Knife Collector's
Club**
C/O Adrienne Escoe
P.O. Box 342
Los Alamitos, CA 90720

**Glass Research Society
of New Jersey**
Wheaton Village
Milville, NJ 08332

**Heart of America
Carnival Glass Assoc.**
C/O Lucille Britt
3048 Tamarek Dr.
Manhattan, KS 66502

**Heisey Collectors of
America, Inc.**
P.O. Box 4367
Newark, OH 43055

Heisey Publications
P.O. Box 102
Plymouth, OH 44865

**International Carnival
Glass Assoc.**
Lee Markley
R.R. #1 P.O. Box 14
Mentone, IN 46539

R. Lalique
11028 Raleigh Ct.
Rockford, IL 61111

Maine Antique Digest
P.O. Box 1429
Waldoboro, ME 04572

**Marble Collector's
Society**
P.O. Box 222
Trumbull, CT 06611

**Morgantown Collectors
of America**
420 1st Ave. N.W.
Plainview, MN 55964

**Mount Washington Art
Glass Society**
P.O. Box 24094
Fort Worth, TX 76124

**National Association of
Avon Collectors**
6100 Walnut, Dept. P
Kansas City, MO 64113

**National Depression
Glass Assoc.**
P.O. Box 69843
Odessa, TX 79769

**The National Duncan
Glass Society**
P.O. Box 965
Washington, PA 15301

**The National Early
American Glass Club**
P.O. Box 8489
Silver Spring, MD 20907

**The National Fenton
Glass Society**
P.O. Box 4008
Marietta, OH 45750

**The National Green-
town Glass Assoc.**
1807 W. Madison St.
Kokomo, IN 46901

**The National Imperial
Glass Collectors Society**
P.O. Box 534
Bellaire, OH 43906

**The National Insulator
Assoc.**
3557 Nicklaus Dr.
Titusville, FL 32780

**The National Milk
Glass Collectors Society**
1113 Birchwood Dr.
Garland, TX 75043

**The National Reamer
Assoc.**
C/O Larry Branstad
R.R. 3 Box 67
Frederic, WI 54837

**The National West-
moreland Glass Collec-
tors Club**
P.O. Box 372
Export, PA 15632

**New England Antiques
Journal**
4 Church St.
Ware, MA 01082

**New England Carnival
Glass Club**
12 Sherwood Dr.
West Hartford, CT
06117

**Ohio Candlewick
Collectors' Club**
613 S. Patterson St.
Gibsonburg, OH 43431

Old Morgantown Glass Collectors' Guild
P.O. Box 894
Morgantown, WV 26507

Pairpoint Cup Plate Collectors of America, Inc.
P.O. Box 52 D
East Weymouth, MA 02189

Paperweight Collectors
P.O. Box 1059
Easthampton, MA 49125

Perfume and Scent Bottle Collectors
2022 E. Charleston Blvd.
Las Vegas, NV 89104

Perfume Bottle Association
P.O. Box 529
Vienna, VA 22183

Phoenix & Consolidated Collectors Association
P.O. Box 81974
Chicago, IL 60681

Rose Bowl Collectors
5214 Route 309
Center Valley, PA 18034

The Shot Glass Club of America
P.O. Box 90404
Flint, MI 48509

The Stretch Glass Society
P.O. Box 770643
Lakewood, OH 44107

Thimble Collectors International
6411 Montego Rd.
Louisville, KY 40228

Three Rivers Depression Era Glass Society
4038 Willett Rd.
Pittsburgh, PA 15227

Tiffin Glass Collectors Club
P.O. Box 554
Tiffin, OH 44883

Toothpick Holder Collectors' Club
Red Arrow Hwy.
P.O. Box 246
Sawyer, MI 49125

Whimsey Glass Club
4544 Cairo Dr.
Whitehall, PA 18052

World's Fair Collectors Society, Inc.
P.O. Box 20806
Sarasota, FL 34238

CHAPTER 5

INSTANT EXPERT QUIZ

To test your general knowledge of glassware, answer the 25 questions below. Be sure to grade yourself—a failing grade only means that you need to read and study a bit more!

NUMBER CORRECT	GRADE	RANK
23–25	A	Glass Master
20–22	B	Glass Expert
15–19	C	Experienced Glass Collector
10–14	D	Glass Novice
0–9	E	Glass Failure

1. What is the rarest and most valuable color in Depression Glass?

2. What are the two major color groups of Carnival Glass?

3. What glass company produced the English Hobnail pattern?

4. What is the most famous island of Venice where glass has been produced for centuries?

5. What company patented Royal Flemish Art Glass?

6. Who or what company is the most noteworthy Czechoslovakian Art Glass producer?

7. What are the three major periods in American glassmaking history?

8. Explain how the cracks are induced in making crackle glass.

9. How do you determine the base color of Carnival Glass?

10. What is the primary coloring agent of Cranberry Glass?

11. Name two producers of Irish Glass other than Waterford.

12. Name the two principal American designers who spawned the Art Glass revolution in the United States.

13. What are the two most popular colors of Depression Glass?

14. Which is more valuable, Amberina or Plated Amberina glassware?

15. What color may older Pressed Glass made with lead turn if exposed to prolonged periods of direct sunlight?

16. What is the most prevalent Carnival colored glassware?

17. What is the pattern name of the oldest and rarest Fire King glassware?

18. Name the two most famous companies associated with American Art Glass lamps.

19. The classical period for paperweights in the mid-nineteenth century occurred in what country?

20. What is the base color along with the three separate trim colors of Fenton's Crest patterned glassware?

21. What is Steuben's most noteworthy colored Art Glass design?

22. Name three famous French Art Glass producers.

23. What kind of Art Glass is often referred to as buttermilk because of its milky yellow coloring?

24. How does Carnival Glass get its oily surface color?

25. What is the key metallic ingredient in Ruby Red glassware?

Answers

1. Black.
2. Bright and pastel.
3. Westmoreland.
4. Murano.
5. Mount Washington.
6. Leo Moser or the Moser Glass Works.
7. Early, Middle, and Brilliant.
8. By plunging hot glass objects into lukewarm or cool water.
9. By looking on the underside of the piece.
10. Gold or gold oxide.
11. Kerry Glass, Tipperary, Galway, Cavan Crystal.
12. Louis Comfort Tiffany and Frederick Carder.
13. Pink and green.
14. Plated Amberina.
15. A light purple or amethyst tinge.
16. Marigold.
17. Philbe Fire King.
18. Tiffany and Handel.
19. France.
20. The base is milk while the trims are green (Emerald Crest), aqua (Aqua Crest), and clear (Silver Crest).
21. Aurene.

22. *Lalique, Baccarat, Clichy, St. Louis, Daum, Gallé, Rousseau.*

23. *Custard.*

24. *By the spraying of metallic salts.*

25. *Gold or gold oxide (the same as Cranberry).*

GLOSSARY

Acid Cut Back: The process of dipping an object into acid for a controlled amount of time in order to achieve a desired cutting depth.

Acid Etching: The process of covering glass with an acid-resistant protective layer, scratching on a design, and then applying hydrofluoric acid to etch the pattern into the glass.

Advertising Glass: A glass vessel displaying information about a manufacturer, company, proprietor, brand, person, establishment, event, and so on.

Agata Glass: Art Glass characterized by mottled purple or brown finishes as a result of alcohol added on top of the color. Agata Glass was produced by the New England Glass Company in the late nineteenth century.

Air Twist: An eighteenth-century English decorating technique where air bubbles were purposefully injected into the base of an object and then pulled down and twisted into a stem.

Albertine Glass: Albertine was produced by the Mount Washington Glass Company in the late nineteenth century. It is characterized by opaque glass and ornate decoration, and was applied primarily to show items such as vases. It is sometimes referred to as Crown Milano.

Alexandrite Glass: Art Glass produced by Thomas Webb in England in the late nineteenth century. It is characterized by various shadings of blue, pink or red, and yellow achieved through several stages of refiring.

Amber: A yellowish-brown colored glass produced by the addition of iron, carbon, and sulfur.

Amberina: Art Glass produced in America in the late nineteenth century. It is characterized by transparent glass that is lightly shaded with light amber at the base and gradually shaded darker to ruby red at the top. Joseph Locke received a patent for Amberina in 1883.

Amelung Glass: High-quality glass made in America in the late eighteenth century by German immigrant John Frederick Amelung.

Amethyst: Purple-colored glass produced by the addition of manganese. Some amethyst glass was made so dark that it is referred to as Black Amethyst.

Animal Dishes: Covered glass dishes or glass objects made in the shapes of various animals (roosters, horses, cats, dogs, elephants, etc.). Animal dishes were very popular from about 1890–1910, a little during the Depression era, and from the 1970s on.

Annealing: A process that toughens glass and eliminates stress by heating and gradually cooling in an annealing oven or lehr.

AOP: An abbreviation for "all-over pattern." All-over patterns generally cover the entire glass object but may be limited to the outside only.

Apricot: A deep yellow or dark amber colored glass.

Art or Art Nouveau Glass: Expensive hand-blown glass with unusual effects of color, shape, and design. Art Glass is primarily ornamental and was most popular from the 1880s to 1920.

Atomizer: *See* Cologne Bottle; Perfume Bottle.

Aurene: Iridescent ornamental Art Glass created by Frederick Carder at the Steuben Glass Works in 1905.

Aventurine: An ancient Egyptian technique of applying small flakes of metal such as gold and copper in colored glass. This technique was popular during the Art Nouveau period.

Baccarat: Fine-quality glass first made in France and Belgium in the late eighteenth century. Baccarat glass was particularly noted for paperweights early on but also produced tableware and other decorative glass. Baccarat Crystal is some of the finest made in the world today.

Ball Stopper: A spherical glass object that rests at the top of glass bottles, jugs, decanters, etc. Its diameter is larger than the mouth of the vessel.

Banana Boat or Dish: A long flat or shallow dish, with sides that are possibly curved upward, with or without a separate base, and used for serving bananas or banana splits.

Base Color: The color of glass before any coating is applied; usually the color of Carnival Glass before it is iridized.

Basket: A glass receptacle with semicircular handle used for foods, decoration, or displaying flowers.

Batch: The mixture of raw materials fused together before heating.

Beading: The process where chips or small relief beads are fused to a glass object in a continuous row.

Bell or Dinner Bell: A hollow device with ringer and single top handle used for summoning or signaling when rung (such as to announce dinnertime).

Best Metal: The highest-quality batch of glass made by a company using the purest ingredients and highest lead content.

Bevel: Slanted or angle cuts usually beginning at the bottom or sides of a glass object (sometimes referred to as flutes at the bottom).

Black Glass: Dark opaque ebony glass created by the combination of oxide of manganese and oxide of iron added to a batch of glass.

Blank: An uncut piece of glass, ordinarily a bowl or vase, that has been specifically made of heavy, high-quality lead glassware.

Blowing: The process of blowing air through a metal tube or blowpipe in order to shape the molten glass blob attached to its end.

Blowpipe: A hollow metal tube used to gather molten glass from the pot and then to blow air through it in order to shape glass.

Bluerina: Art Glass made in America in the late nine-teenth century that is very similar to Amberina; only the colors gradually meld from blue at the base to Amberina at the top.

Bohemian Glass: German-made glass in the seven-teenth century characterized by ornate decoration, heavy cutting, and bright colors.

Bottle: A glass container with a narrow neck and mouth; may or may not have a handle. Bottles come in all shapes and sizes and can be made of other materials.

Bowl: A concave glass vessel, hemispherical in shape, used for holding liquids and other foods; (made in soup, salad, serving, cereal, berry, vegetable, and many other shapes and sizes. The bowl of a wine or stemmed beverage glass is the portion that holds the liquid.

Brandy Glass: A short rounded glass with a foot and very tiny stem; shorter but wider as compared to a rounded wine glass.

Bread and Butter Plate: A round flat object that is usu-ally 6 inches in diameter.

Bride's Basket: A fancy bowl held within a silver or sil-verplated frame. Bride's baskets were popular wed-ding gifts during the Brilliant Period after they debuted at the World's Columbian Exposition in Chicago in 1893.

Brilliant Period: The era of American handmade glass-ware from 1880 to 1915 characterized by fine cutting, engraving, polishing, and fancy patterns.

Bristol Glass: Crystal, colored, and milk glass items pro-duced in several factories in Bristol, England, in the seventeenth and eighteenth centuries.

Burmese Glass: Glass objects characterized by various light opaque shadings in pastel colors of pink, yellow, and white produced with the addition of uranium. It was first created by the Mount Washington Glass Company in the late nineteenth century and then pro-duced by others.

Butter Dish: A glass dish that is ordinarily flat or footed, with or without glass dome or rectangular cover, and used for serving butter, margarine, or other spreads.

Butter Tub: A glass vessel shaped as a small bucket or pail (usually smaller than an ice bucket) with or without semicircular handle, and used for serving butter balls.

Cake Plate: A large flat or footed glass plate, usually round in shape, and used for holding cakes.

Calcite Glass: A brightly colored cream-white colored glass that resembles the mineral calcite (calcite is not used in its manufacture). Calcite glass was first produced by Frederick Carder at the Steuben Glass Works in the early twentieth century.

Cameo Engraving: An engraving process where the background is carved away to leave the design in relief (*see* Relief Cutting).

Canary Yellow: A bright yellow colored glass similar to amber colored glass (also made with various amounts of iron, carbon, and sulfur).

Candelabrum: A branched candlestick with several sockets for holding candles. (Plural: candelabra.)

Candy Dish: An open shallow bowl-like glass receptacle used for serving candy; may or may not be footed.

Candy Jar: A tall, wide-mouthed glass receptacle with cover used for serving candy; may or may not be footed.

Carafe: A large glass bottle with stopper used for serving beverages (usually water or wine).

Card Tray: A flat glass object, usually rectangular in shape, with possibly a center handle and two separate sections, and used for holding standard-size playing cards.

Carnival Glass: Pressed glassware with a fired-on iridescent finish made in the United States 1905–1925 (reproductions were produced later, beginning in the 1960s).

Cased Glass: Nineteenth-century glass that was blown in multiple layers of separate colors. The glass was then decorated by cutting away all or part of these layers.

Casserole Dish: A deep round, oblong, or square dish, with or without cover, with or without handles or tabs, and used to bake as well as serve food.

Cast Glass: Glass made in simple molds and then surface-ground with polishing wheels fed by abrasives.

Castor Set: A set of glass serving objects held on glass or metal trays. These objects might include small pitchers, cruets, small jars, salt and pepper shakers, and other small dishes.

Centerpiece: A large circular or oval fancy glass bowl used as an adornment in the center of a table.

Champagne Glass: A tall glass with foot and stem with a large round but shallow bowl.

Chalice: A fancy drinking vessel with large rounded bowl of various sizes and shapes (may or may not be stemmed).

Chandelier: An ornate branched glass lighting fixture suspended from a ceiling.

Cheese and Cracker Dish: A serving dish with two levels (two-tiered), one for holding cheese or a cheese ball (usually the upper part), and the other for crackers.

Cheese Dish: A glass dish that is ordinarily flat or footed with a separate glass cover (usually dome-shaped) that is used for serving cheese. Note that cheese dishes are a little larger than butter dishes.

Chintz: A style of glass patented by A. Douglas Nash. It was characterized by colored ribbed, striped, or swirled glass marvered into opaque, opalescent, and transparent glass. The process was expensive and difficult, since the separate colors often ran together.

Chocolate Glass: A variegated opaque glass that shades from dark brown to light tan. It was first developed by the Indiana Tumbler & Goblet Company and is sometimes mistakenly referred to as caramel slag.

Clambroth or Clam Broth: Grayish-colored, semi-transparent glass.

Claret Glass: A tall glass with foot and stem with a large round deep bowl specifically designed for serving claret wine.

Cluthra: An Art Glass form developed by Steuben in 1920. It is characterized by a cloudy opaque design permeated by varying sized bubbles. Offshoots of the basic design were produced by others, such as Kimble.

Coaster: A very shallow or flat container used to place other glass objects upon (such as tumblers) to protect the surface beneath it (e.g., tabletops, counters).

Cobalt Blue: Metallic coloring agent producing the most powerful deep dark blue color within glass.

Cocktail Glass: A tall glass with foot, stem, and an angled or straight-edged bowl.

Coin Glass: Originally in the eighteenth and nineteenth centuries, a tumbler or tankard with a real coin visibly placed in the foot or stem. Later twentieth-century versions contain glass coin replicas inscribed within the glass.

Cologne Bottle: A small glass receptacle with narrow neck and stopper used for holding colognes or perfumes.

Compote or Comport: A glass serving bowl that may contain a base, stem, or foot/feet used for serving candy, fruits, or nuts. Compotes are most commonly referred to as raised candy dishes.

Console Bowl: A large concave glass vessel, hemispherical in shape, and used as a centerpiece or for serving large items. Console bowls are sometimes accompanied by a pair of matching candlesticks.

Cookie Jar: A tall, wide-mouthed, canister-shaped glass receptacle (larger than a candy jar), with cover, without feet or stems, and used for holding cookies.

Copper Wheel Engraving: Process of hand engraving by holding a glass to a revolving copper wheel which instantly cuts through the surface. Some of the best glass ever produced was done by highly skilled copper-wheel engravers who kept the cutting pattern in their minds while altering the cutting with rubbing oil continuously for hours on end.

Coral: Various shadings of yellow to red layers applied to glass objects with opaque-colored bases.

Coralene Glass: Art Glass that was first made in nineteenth-century Europe and then in America. It is characterized by enamel and colored or opaque glass drops applied to raised branches that resembled coral.

Cordial Glass: A miniature wineglass with foot, stem, and bowl of small capacity.

Core-Forming: Process of glassmaking by spinning glass around a core.

Cracker Jar: A tall wide-mouthed canister-shaped glass receptacle with cover used for holding crackers.

Crackling: A decorating technique applied to glassware by plunging a hot object into cold water to induce cracks, and then re-forming the piece within a mold.

Cranberry Glass: First developed in England in the nineteenth century; cranberry glass is characterized by a light red tint (the color of cranberries) produced by the addition of gold dust. Originally it was a cheaper substitute for ruby red, but now the name is applied to any glass made of the cranberry color.

Creamer: A small glass cuplike vessel, ordinarily with handle, and used for serving cream (with coffee and tea; usually paired with a sugar dish).

Crown Milano: *See* Albertine Glass.

Cruet: A small glass bottle or decanter with top used to hold a condiment such as oil, vinegar, or salad dressing for use at the table.

Crystal: Colorless glass with a high lead content.

Cuspidor: A fancy glass vessel or receptacle used for containing saliva (*see* Spittoon).

Custard Glass: A yellowish-colored or yellowish-cream-colored opaque glass (the color of custard) first developed in the early 1900s.

Cut Glass: Heavy flint glass cut with geometric patterns into the glass with grinding wheels and abrasives. The design is then further smoothed and polished. Cutting originated in Germany and then was introduced in the United States in the late eighteenth century.

Cut Velvet: Colored Art Glass consisting of two fused, mold-blown layers that leaves the outer surface design raised in relief.

Decal: A picture, design, or label from specially prepared paper that is transferred to glass, usually by heating.

Decanter: An ornamental or fancy glass bottle with

cover or stopper, with or without handles, and used for serving wine or other alcoholic beverages.

Delphite: A lightly colored pale blue opaque glass; it is sometimes referred to as Blue Milk Glass.

Demitasse: Matching cups and saucers that are much smaller (half size or less) than their ordinary counterparts. Note that demitasse cups and saucers are still slightly larger than those found in children's miniature teasets.

Depression Glass: Mass-produced, inexpensive, and primarily machine-made glass dinner sets and giftware in clear and many colors produced in America between 1920 and 1940.

Diamond Point Engraving: Hand cutting or machine cutting of glass with a diamond point tool (note that hardened metal shaped by heat treating to a sharp point has since replaced the more expensive diamonds for machine cutting).

Diatreta Glass: Art Glass made by applying tiny pieces of ornamental glass in patterns to other larger glass objects. This process was first developed by Frederick Carder in the early 1900s.

Domino Tray: A serving dish with a built-in container for cream and surrounding area specifically designed for holding sugar cubes.

Dram Glass: Small English or Irish glasses made of metal used for drinking a single measure of strong liquor. Most were made between 1750 and 1850 and imported to the United States.

Dresser Set: A set of glass bath or bedroom objects held on a matching tray. These objects might include perfume or cologne bottles; jars; and tiny boxes for gloves, hair- or hatpins, and jewelry.

Ebony Glass: Another name for black or very dark black opaque glass.

Eggcup or Egg Holder: A small cuplike vessel, without handle, with room enough to hold a single egg. Occasionally, double egg holders have been made (room for two eggs).

Embossing: Mold blown or pressed glassware where the design is applied directly upon the object from the mold. Embossed patterns are usually somewhat in relief.

Emerald Green: A deep, powerful green color (the color of the gemstone emerald) usually made with chromium and iron.

Enameling: A liquid medium similar to paint applied to glassware and then permanently fused onto the object by heating.

Encased Overlay: A single or double overlay design further encased in clear glass.

Engraving: The decoration of glass applied by holding the piece against the edge of revolving wheels made of stone, copper, or other materials.

Epergne: A large table centerpiece that includes a large bowl surrounded by several matching smaller dishes.

Etching: *See* Acid Etching.

Ewer: A round glass jug-like object, with or without foot, and usually containing a long handle and spout.

Favrile: An American Art Nouveau style of glass created by Louis Comfort Tiffany in the late nineteenth century. The original pieces are often referred to as Tiffany Favrile.

Figurine: A small individual etched or molded statue (or figure).

Finger Bowl: A small concave glass vessel, usually circular and shallow in shape, and used for rinsing fingers at the table.

Finial: A crowning ornament or decorative knob found most often in stemware and at the top of glass covers.

Fire Polishing: Reheating a finished piece of glass at the glory hole in order to remove tool marks (more commonly replaced with acid polishing).

Fired-On: Finishing colors that are baked on or fused by heating on to the outer surface of glass objects.

Fired-On Iridescence: A finish applied to glass by adding metallic salts, after which the glass is refired.

Flashed-On Iridescence: A finish applied to glass by dipping hot glass into a solution of metallic salts.

Flashing: A very thin coating of a different color from that of the base color (thinner than a casing or an overlay).

Flask: A glass container with narrow neck and mouth, with stopper or cover, and used for carrying alcoholic beverages.

Flint Glass: The American term for fine glassware made in the nineteenth century. A name for lead glass, though original experimenters used powdered flints as substitutes for lead oxides.

Floret or Florette: A slice from a large cane of several colored rods arranged (usually concentrically) to form a floral pattern.

Flower Bowl: A large shallow concave hemispherical container used for holding or floating flowers with relatively short stems.

Fluting: Vertically cut decoration in long narrow or parallel sections such as bevels (usually wheel-cut but sometimes molded).

Folded Foot: The turned-over edge of the foot of a wineglass or similar glass object to give added strength to the vessel.

Foot: The part of a glass other than the base on which it rests.

Forest Green: A dark green color not as deep or rich as emerald green, first made in the late 1930s and early 1940s by the Hazel Atlas Glass Company, which patented the name. The term has been applied to glassware made by other companies in the same color.

Frances Ware: Mold blown tableware consisting of amber color, fluted rims, and hobnail patterns; it was produced by Hobbs, Brocunier & Company in the 1880s.

Free-Blown Glass: An ancient technique of hand-blowing glass by highly skilled craftsmen without the use of molds.

Frog: A small but thick and heavy glass object, usually

round or domed, and containing perforations, holes, or spikes, for holding flowers in place within a vase.

Frosted Glass: A light opalescence or cloudy coloring of a batch of glass using tin, zinc, or an allover acid etching, as in Depression Glass. A frosted coating can also be applied on the surface of clear or crystal glass by spraying on white acid (a solution of ammonium bifluoride).

Full Lead Crystal: Colorless glass containing a minimum of 30 percent lead content.

Gather: A blob of molten glass attached to the end of a blowpipe, pontil, or gathering iron.

Gilding: An applied decorating technique with gold enamels or paints to finished glass objects.

Glass: A hard, brittle, artificial substance made by fusing silicates (sand) with an alkali (soda or potash) and sometimes with metallic oxides (lead oxide or lime).

Glass House: The building that contains the glass-melting furnaces and in which the actual handling and shaping of molten glass takes place.

Glass Picture: A design that is ordinarily etched on flat sheets or flat pieces of glass.

Glove Box: A rectangular glass object, with or without cover, used specifically on dressing tables or vanities for holding gloves.

Goblet: A drinking vessel with a large bowl of various sizes and shapes that rests on a stemmed foot.

Gone With the Wind Lamp: A kerosene or electric table lamp containing a glass base with a round, globe-shaped glass shade.

Grapefruit Bowl: A concave glass vessel, usually circular in shape, ordinarily with a wide foot, and used for serving half a grapefruit.

Green Glass: The natural color of ordinary alkaline- or lime-based glassware usually produced by iron present in the sand.

Grill Plate: A large individual or serving plate with divisions (similar to relish dishes, only larger).

Ground: The background or base glass object on which decorations are applied.

Half Lead Crystal: Colorless glass containing a minimum of 24 percent lead content (lower-quality than full lead crystal).

Hand-Blown Glass: Glass formed and shaped with a blowpipe and other hand-manipulated tools without the use of molds.

Hand Cooler: A solid ovoid or small glass object originally developed in ancient Rome for ladies to cool their hands. Later, hand coolers were also used by ladies when being wooed or for darning.

Hand-Pressed Glass: Glass that is made in hand-operated mechanical presses.

Hat or Hat Vase: A whimsical glass object in the shape of an upside down head covering or top hat. The space where one's head would usually rest is often used for flowers or for holding tiny objects.

Highball Glass: A tall narrow tumbler of at least 4-ounce capacity used for mixed drinks.

Hobnail: A pressed or cut pattern in glassware resembling small raised knobs referred to as "hobs" or "prunts." The name originated in England from the large heads of hobnail fasteners.

Holly Amber: A type of Art Glass made only in 1903 by the Indiana Tumbler and Goblet Company; it is a pressed design characterized by creamy opalescent to brown amber shading (golden agate) with pressed holly leaves.

Honey Dish: A tiny flat or shallow dish used for serving honey.

Horseradish Jar: A small to medium-sized covered glass receptacle used for serving horseradish.

Humidor: A glass jar or case used, for holding cigars, in which the air is kept properly humidified.

Ice Blue: A very light shade or tint of transparent blue glass (the color of ice).

Ice Bucket or Tub: A glass vessel shaped as a medium-sized bucket or pail, with or without semicircular handle, and used for holding ice.

Ice Cream Plate: A small flat glass plate, usually round in shape, and used for serving a single scoop of ice cream.

Ice Cream Tray: A large shallow or flat glass container used for serving ice cream.

Ice Glass: A type of Art Glass characterized by a rough surface that resembles cracked ice.

Ice Lip: A rim at the top of a pitcher that prevents ice from spilling out of the spout when it is tilted or poured.

Incising: The technique of cutting or engraving designs into the surface of glass.

Inkwell: A small but heavy glass container used for holding ink (originally for quill pens).

Intaglio: An engraving or cutting made below the surface of glass so that the impression left from the design leaves an image in relief.

Intarsia: The name given to a type of glass produced by Steuben in the 1920s. It is characterized by a core of colored glass blown between layers of clear glass, then decorated by etching into mosaic patterns.

Iridescence: A sparkling rainbow-colored finish applied to the exterior of glass objects that is produced by adding metallic salts.

Iridized: Glass that has been coated with iridescence.

Ivory: A cream or off-white colored opaque glass (the color of ivory).

Ivrene: A white opaque glass with a light pearl-like iridescent coating; originally made by Steuben.

Jack-in-the-Pulpit: A style of vase made to resemble the American woodland flower. It usually consists of a circular base, thin stem, and a large open ruffled bloom at the top.

Jadeite or Jade-ite: A pale lime-colored opaque green glass (the color of jade).

Jardiniere: An ornamental glass stand or vase-like vessel used for holding plants or flowers.

Jelly Dish or Tray: A small flat or shallow dish used for serving jelly, jam, marmalade, and other preserves.

Jennyware: The nickname for kitchenware glass made by the Jeannette Glass Company.

Jewel Box: A glass receptacle, usually rectangular in shape, with or without cover, and used for storing jewelry.

Jug: A large deep glass vessel; usually with a wide mouth, pouring spout, and handle; and used for storing liquids.

Juice Glass: A short narrow glass tumbler, with or without foot, with capacity of 3 to 6 ounces, and used for drinking fruit and vegetable juices.

Kew Blas: A name given to a type of opaque Art Glass produced by the Union Glass Company in the 1890s. The primary color is brown with various shadings of brown and green.

Kick: A small indentation in the bottom of a glass object.

Kiln: An oven used for firing or refiring glass objects.

Knife Rest: A small, thick barbell-shaped glass object used to hold knife blades off the table when eating.

Knop: An ornamental ball-shaped swelling on the stem of stemmed glassware such as wineglasses.

Lace Glass: A mid-sixteenth-century Venetian-styled glass characterized by transparent threaded designs layered on the sides of various glass objects.

Lacy Pressed Glass: A mid-nineteenth-century American style of pressed glass characterized by an overall angular and round braiding pattern.

Lamp Shade: Glass coverings that shelter lights in order to reduce glare. At times, large glass bowls are converted to lamp shades by drilling holes in their center to attach them above the light.

Latticino: A sixteenth-century Venetian-styled glass characterized by white opaque glass threads applied to clear glass objects.

Lava Glass: A style of Art Glass invented by Louis Comfort Tiffany characterized by dark blue and gray opaque hues (the color of cooled lava) and some-times coated with gold or silver decorations.

Layered Glass: Glass objects with overlapping levels or layers of glass.

Lead Crystal: Crystal or colorless glass made with a high lead content (*see* Full Lead Crystal; Half Lead Crystal).

Lily Pad: A name given to a decoration applied to glass objects characterized by a superimposed layer of glass. Several styles of leaves (including lily pads), flowers, and stems were then designed on this layer.

Lime Glass: A glass formula developed by William Leighton as a substitute for lead glass. Calcined lime-stone was substituted for lead, which made glass cheaper to produce. Lime glass also cools faster than lead glassware but is lighter and less resonant.

Lotz or Loetz Glass: Art Nouveau glass produced by Johann Lotz of Austria in the late nineteenth and early twentieth centuries.

Loving Cup: A glass drinking vessel, with or without foot, and usually containing three handles.

Low Relief: An engraving process where the background is cut away to a very low degree (*see* Relief Cutting).

Marbled Glass: Glass objects with single or multiple color swirls made to resemble marble.

Mary Gregory: Clear and colored glassware (commonly pastel pink) decorated with white enamel designs of one or more boys and/or girls playing in Victorian scenes. Mary Gregory actually worked as a decorator for the Boston & Sandwich Glass Company from 1870 to 1880, but it is not known if she ever painted her namesake glass.

Mercury Glass: Glass objects characterized by two outer layers of clear glass with an inner layer of mercury or silver nitrate between them.

Merese: An ornamental notch or knob between the stem and bowl of stemware.

Metal: A term used by chemists for a batch of glass (*see* Best Metal).

Milk Glass: A semi-opaque opalescent glass colored by a compound of arsenic or calcined bones or tin. The result is a white color resembling milk.

Millefiori: An eighteenth-century European-style paperweight made with several different-colored glass rods together in a pattern and then covered with an extremely thick outer layer of glass.

Miter-Cut Engraving: Glass cut with a sharp groove on a V-edged wheel.

Moil: Waste glass left on the blowpipe or pontil.

Mold: A wooden or iron form used to shape glass. Pattern or half-molds are used before glass has totally expanded. Full or three-part molds are used to give identical or same-size shapes to glassware. (Old English spelling of mold is "mould.")

Molded Glass: Blown or melted glass that is given its final shape by the use of molds.

Monart Glass: An Art Glass of Spain characterized by opaque and clear marble swirls.

Monax: A partially opaque or nearly transparent cream-colored or off-white glass first produced and named by the MacBeth-Evans Glass Company.

Moss Agate: An Art Glass first created by Steuben characterized by red, brown, and other swirled or marble-like colors.

Mother-of-Pearl: An Art Glass technique produced by trapping air between layers of glass.

Mustard Dish or Jar: A small flat or shallow dish, with or without cover, used specifically for serving mustard. If lids are present they may or may not contain an opening for a matching spoon.

Napkin Ring: A small circular glass band used for holding a table napkin.

Napoli: Glass objects that are completely covered with gold or gold enamels, both inside and out. Additional decorations may be applied to the gold covering.

Nappy: An open shallow serving bowl without a rim that may contain one or two handles.

Near Cut: Pressed glass patterns similar to designs of hand-decorated cut glass.

Neck: The part of a glass vessel such as a bottle, jug, or similar article between the body and mouth.

Needle Etching: A process of etching glass by machine. Fine lines are cut by a machine through a wax coating upon glass and then hydrofluoric acid is applied to etch the pattern into the glass.

New Carnival: Reproduction iridescent glass made since 1962, sometimes with the original Carnival Glass molds.

Obsidian: A mineral that resembles dark glass; black glass is sometimes referred to as obsidian glass.

Off-Hand Glass: Glass objects such as whimsies, art pieces, or other novelty items created by glassmakers from leftover or scrap glass.

Oil Bottle: A glass receptacle with top used for serving vinegar or other salad oils (*see* Cruet).

Old Gold: A deep amber stain or amber applied to glass made to resemble gold.

Onyx Glass: A dark-colored glass with streaking of white or other colors made by mixing molten glass with various color mediums.

Opalescence: A milky or cloudy coloring of glass. Opalescent coating is usually made by adding tin or zinc. Opalescent glass was first made by Frederick Carder at Steuben in the early twentieth century.

Opal Glass: An opalescent opaque-like white milk glass usually produced with tin (*see* Milk Glass).

Opaline Glass: An opaque Art Glass, pressed or blown, that was first developed by Baccarat in the early nineteenth century.

Opaque Glass: Glass that is so dark in color that it does not transmit light (milk glass, for example).

Ormolu: A decorative object usually made of brass, bronze, or gold applied to glass objects (such as a knob on stemware).

Overlay Glass: The technique of placing one colored glass on top of another, with designs cut through the outermost layer only.

Overshot Glass: A type of glass with a very rough or jagged finish produced by rolling molten glass objects into crushed glass.

Parfait: A tall, narrow glass with short stem and foot used for serving ice cream.

Pâte de Verre: Meaning "paste of glass"; it is an ancient material made from powdered glass or glasslike substances that is formed into a pastelike material by heating and then hardened. The resulting form is carved, painted, or applied with other decorations.

Pattern Glass: Glass produced by mechanically pressing it into molds. The design is cut directly in the mold.

Pattern-Molded Glass: Glass that is first impressed into small molds and then removed and blown to a larger size (blown-molded).

Peach Blow Glass: An American Art Glass produced by several companies in the late nineteenth century. It is characterized by multicolor opaque shades such as cream, white, pink, orange, and red.

Pearline Glass: A late-nineteenth-century-style Art Glass with color variance of pale to deep dark opaque blues.

Pearl Ornaments: A molded glass pattern consisting of diamonds, squares, and other diagonal bandings.

Peking Cameo: Cameo engraved glass first made in China in the late seventeenth century in the city of Peking. It was made to resemble more expensive Chinese porcelain.

Peloton Glass: A style of Art Glass first made by Wilhelm Kralik in Bohemia in 1880. It is produced by rolling colored threads into colored glass directly after it was removed from the furnace.

Perfume Bottle: A tiny glass receptacle with narrow neck and stopper used for holding perfume.

Photochromic Glass: A glass developed by the Corning Glass Works in Corning, New York, in 1964. When the glass is exposed to ultraviolet radiation such as sunlight, it darkens; when the radiation is removed, the glass clears.

Pickle Castor: A glass jar held within a silver or silver-plated metal frame, usually with handle and matching spoon, and used for serving pickles. These jars were most popular during the Victorian Period.

Pigeon Blood: A color of glass characterized by brown highlighting over ruby red.

Pin Tray: A tiny flat or shallow glass dish used for holding hairpins.

Pitcher: A wide-mouthed glass vessel, usually with spout and handle, with or without lip, and used for pouring or serving liquids.

Pittsburgh Glass: High-quality pressed glass made in America by several companies in and around Pittsburgh, Pennsylvania, in the late eighteenth and nineteenth centuries.

Plate: A flat glass object, usually round in shape (occasionally square or oval), used for serving dinner, lunch, desserts, and other foods.

Plated Glass: Glass that is covered by more than one layer; usually clear glass that is dipped or completely covered with colored glass.

Platinum Band: A metal silver-colored trim applied to rims or by banding around glass objects (made of genuine platinum).

Platonite: A heat-resistant opaque white-colored glass first produced and named by Hazel Atlas in the 1930s and 1940s.

Polychromic Glass: Glass characterized by two or more colors.

Pomona Glass: An Art Glass created by applying or dipping the object into acid to produce a mottled, frosted appearance. It was first developed by Joseph Locke at the New England Glass Company in the late nineteenth century.

Powder Jar: A small glass receptacle, usually with cover, and used for holding various body powders. Powder jars are ordinarily part of dresser sets.

Preserve Dish: A small flat or shallow dish, with or without foot, and used for serving jelly, jam, and other fruit preserves.

Pressed Glass: Hot molten glass mechanically forced into molds under pressure (an important American invention in the 1820s was the hand press).

Pressing: The process begins with molten glass poured into a mold, which forms the outer surface of an object. A plunger lowered into the mass leaves a smooth center with a patterned exterior. Flat plates and dishes are formed in a base mold, and an upper section folds down to mold the top (like a waffle iron).

Prism Cutting: Cut glass made with long horizontal grooves or lines that usually meet at a common point.

Prunts: A German decoration or ornamentation characterized by small glass knobs or drops attached to drinking vessels; the term later became another name for hobs on hobnail-patterned glass.

Puff Box: A small square, rectangular, or circular glass container with cover used on dressing tables or vanities for holding powders.

Pumice: Volcanic rock that is ground into powder and is used for polishing glass objects.

Pyrex: A type of glass created by Corning Glass in 1912. It contains oxide of boron, which makes the glass extremely heat-resistant. (Sometimes referred to as borosilicate glass.)

Quartz Glass: An Art Glass consisting of a wide variety of colors and shades created by Steuben (designed to imitate the appearance of quartz).

Quezal Glass: An iridescent semi-opaque imitation of Tiffany's Favrile Art Glass made by the Quezal Art Glass & Decoration Company in the early twentieth century.

Quilling: A wavy pattern applied to glass by repeated workings with pincers.

Range Sets: Kitchenware glass sets developed during the Depression period. Items might include canisters, flour jars, sugar jars, and shakers.

Ratafia Glass: A cordial glass used to serve the liquor ratafia.

Reamer: A juice extractor with a ridge and pointed center rising in a shallow dish, usually circular in shape.

Reeding: A decorating technique applied with very fine threads or tiny ropelike strings of glass. The strings are usually colored and applied in a variety of patterns.

Refrigerator Dish: Stackable square or rectangular covered glass containers of various sizes used for storing foods in the refrigerator.

Relief Cutting: A difficult and expensive method of cutting glass by designing the outline on the surface and then cutting away the background. The design is then raised in relief similar to that of cameo engraving.

Relish Dish: A small to medium-sized shallow glass serving tray with divisions, usually rectangular or oval in shape; it may contain one or two handles.

Resonance: The sound that results when a glass object is struck; sometimes used as a test for crystal, though other types of glass resonate with similar sounds.

Reverse Painting: Designs painted on the back side of glass that appear in proper perspective when viewed from the front.

Rib Mold: A pattern mold for bowls, bottles, tumblers, and so on, that is marked with heavy vertical lines or ribbing.

Rigaree: A narrow vertical band decoration applied to glass in various colors.

Ringtree: A glass object in the shape of a miniature tree with knobs that taper upward (the knobs are used to hold finger rings).

Roaster: A deep round, oblong, or angled dish, with or without cover, with or without handles, and used to bake or cook foods.

Rod: A thin solid cylinder or small stick of glass. Many are used together to form a cane.

Rolled Edge: A curved lip or circular base on which glass objects may turn over or rotate.

Rope Edge: A twirled threadlike design usually applied around the edge of glass objects.

Rose: A deep red cranberry-colored glass with the color applied by staining or flashing (not as deep or as dark as ruby red).

Rose Bowl: A small round concave glass vessel usually with three feet (tri-footed), with a small opening in the center for holding a single flower or a few flowers.

Royal Flemish Glass: An Art Glass made by the Mount Washington Glass Works characterized by a raised gilding decoration and light staining.

Rubina Glass: Glass that gradually changes in color from crystal at the bottom to a cranberry or rose color at the top.

Rubina Verde: Glass that gradually changes in color from a light yellow-green at the bottom to a cranberry or rose color at the top.

Ruby Red: A gold metallic coloring agent that produces the most powerful red color within glass.

Sachet Jar: A small glass receptacle, with or without cover, used for holding perfumed powders for scenting clothes and linens.

Salad Plate: A flat glass object, usually round in shape, ordinarily about 7 to 7½″ in diameter (slightly smaller than a lunch plate) and used for serving salads.

Salt Cellar: A small open bowl, with or without foot, used for sprinkling salt on food before the development of shakers. It may or may not have a matching spoon.

Salver: A large platter or tray used for serving food or beverages.

Sandblasting: An American-developed process where the design on a piece of glass is coated with a protective layer and then the exposed surfaces that remain are sandblasted with a pressurized gun to create the design.

Sandwich Glass: An American pressed glass produced in the Eastern United States in the nineteenth century. It was a substitute for more expensive hand-cut crystal glass.

Sandwich Server: A large platter or serving tray with an open or closed center handle.

Satin Glass: An American Art Glass characterized by a smooth lustrous appearance obtained by giving layers of colored glass an allover acid vapor bath.

Sauce Boat: A glass oblong bowl-shaped vessel, usually with a handle on each end, used for serving sauces or gravy.

Sauce Dish: A small, usually flat or shallow dish, with or without handles, possibly footed, and used for serving condiments or sauces.

Saucer: A small flat or shallow plate, usually with an indentation for a matching cup.

Scent Bottle: *see* Cologne Bottle; Perfume Bottle.

Sconce: A glass candlestick bracket with one or more sockets for holding candles.

Shaker: A small glass upright container, usually cylindrical or angular in shape, with metal or plastic covers containing tiny holes, and used for sprinkling salt, pepper, and other spices on foods.

Sham: A very thin, fragile glass tumbler.

Sherbet: A small footed dish, with or without a small stem, and used for serving desserts such as pudding, ice cream, and Jell-O.

Sherry Glass: A tall glass with foot and stem with a shallow angled or straight-edged bowl.

Shot Glass: A small whiskey tumbler with a capacity of at least one ounce but no more than two; and a height of at least $1\frac{3}{4}''$ but strictly less than $3''$.

Silveria Glass: The technique of rolling an extremely thin layer of silver over glass and then blowing it, which shatters the silver into glittery decorative flecks.

Silverina: A type of Art Glass created by Steuben in the early twentieth century using particles of silver and mica applied to the glass object.

Slag Glass: A type of glass made with various scrap metals, including lead, that was first produced in England in the mid-nineteenth century.

Souvenir Glass: Glass objects decorated with a variety of techniques (enameled, painted, transferred, embossed, etc.) depicting cities, states, countries, advertising, tourist attractions, and so on.

Spangled Glass: A late-nineteenth-century American Art Glass made with flakes of mica in the clear glass inner layer and then overlaid by transparent colored glass. The majority of items produced in this style were glass baskets with fancy decorated handles and rims.

Spatter Glass: An opaque white or colored glass produced in both England and America in the late nineteenth century. The exterior is sometimes mottled with large spots of colored glass.

Spittoon: A fancy glass vessel or receptacle used for containing saliva (or spit, hence the name spittoon). Spittoons are sometimes referred to as cuspidors.

Spoon Dish: A flat or shallow glass object, rectangular or oval in shape, used for holding dessert spoons horizontally.

Spooner or Spoon Holder: A tall cylinder-shaped glass vessel, with or without handles, and used for holding dessert spoons vertically.

Sprayed-On Iridescence: Adding iridescence to glass by spraying it with particles of metallic salts.

Spun Glass: Glass threading that was originally spun by hand upon a revolving wheel. Glass fibers are automatically spun by machine today.

Stained Glass: An imitation colored glass created by painting clear glass with metallic stains or transparent paints.

Star Holly: A milk glass design created by the Imperial Glass Corporation in the early 1900s. It was made to duplicate pressed English Wedgwood Glass and was characterized by intertwined holly leaves raised in relief with background color mattes of blue, green, or coral.

Stem: The cylindrical support connecting the foot and

bowl of glass vessels (these vessels include all types of stemware—goblets, wineglasses, compotes, etc.).

Striped Glass: An American Art Glass from the late nineteenth century characterized by wavy bands of contrasting colors.

Sugar: A small glass cup-like vessel, which may or may not have handles, and used for serving sugar (often paired with a creamer for serving tea).

Sugar Shaker: A small glass upright container, usually cylindrical or angular in shape, with metal or plastic covers containing holes, and used for sprinkling sugar on various foods (larger in size than typical salt and pepper shakers).

Sunset-Glow Glass: An early (eighteenth-century) European milk or opalescent white colored glass.

Superimposed Decoration: A glass decoration separate from the object that it is applied to.

Sweetmeat Dish or Compote: A small flat or shallow tray or bowl-like glass object used for serving sweetmeat hors d'oeuvres.

Syrup Pitcher: A small wide-mouthed vessel, with spout, handle, and hinged metal lid, and used for pouring syrup.

Tankard: A large drinking vessel, somewhat straight-edged, with a single handle that may or may not contain a hinged lid (as in steins, the lid and handle may be made of metal).

Tazza: An unusually wide dessert cup or serving plate, with or without handles, mounted on a stemmed foot.

Tea Caddy: A large wide-mouthed glass canister with cover used for storing tea bags or loose tea.

Teal: A bluish-green colored glass (a little darker than ultramarine).

Thread Circuit: A decorative pattern applied with rope-like strings or twists of glass. The strings or threads are often colored and applied in concentric circles or other symmetrical patterns.

Thumbprint: A decorative style usually made by pressing in the form of oval-shaped shallow depressions arranged in rows. Several variations of the basic thumbprint pattern exist (almond thumbprint, diamond thumbprint, etc.).

Tidbit Tray: A tiered dish with a pole connecting two or more levels. The pole usually runs through the center and the size of the levels gradually decreases as they go up.

Topaz: A mineral used as a coloring agent to produce a bright yellow color within glass.

Trailing: The process of pulling out a thread of glass and applying it to the surface of a glass object in spiral or other string designs.

Transfers: A complete design printed on a paper backing that is removed from the backing, applied to glassware, and then fired on in a special enameling lehr.

Translucent: Glass which transmits or diffuses light so that objects lying beyond cannot be seen clearly through it.

Transparent: Glass that transmits light without appreciable scattering so that objects lying beyond are clearly visible.

Tray: A flat glass object, usually oval or rectangular in shape, used for holding or serving various items.

Trivet: A glass plate, usually tri-footed, used under a hot dish to protect the surface (e.g. tabletop) beneath it.

Tumbler: A drinking vessel ordinarily without foot, stem, or handle, and containing a pointed or convex base.

Tumble Up: An inverted glass set for a dresser or night-stand that usually includes a water bottle and other items such as a tray and tumblers.

Ultramarine: A bluish-green aqua color produced by the mineral lazulite or from a mixture of kaolin, soda ash, sulfur, and charcoal.

Urn: An ornamental glass vase with or without pedestal (may or may not have handles); also a closed glass vessel with spigot used for serving liquids.

Vasa Murrhina: An American nineteenth-century Art Glass characterized by an inner layer of colored glass that has powdered metals or mica added for decoration.

Vase: A round or angled glass vessel, usually with a depth greater than its width, and used for holding flowers.

Vaseline Glass: Glass made with a small amount of uranium, which imparts a light greenish-yellow color (a greasy appearance like Vaseline).

Venetian Glass: Clear and colored glassware produced in Venice, Italy, and the surrounding area (especially the island of Murano) from the thirteenth century to the present.

Victorian Glass: English-made glass from about the 1820s through the 1940s characterized by colors, opalescence, opaqueness, art glass, and unusual designs and shapes; named for Queen Victoria (1837–1901).

Water Bottle: A glass container with narrow neck and mouth, usually without a handle, used for drinking water or other liquids.

Wear Marks: Tiny barely visible scratches on the base, foot, or rim which indicate normal wear and tear through years of use. Glass with wear marks is usually not considered mint glassware but it holds much more value than damaged glass.

Whimsy: A small unique decorative glass object made to display a particular glassmaker's skill (sometimes called a frigger).

Wineglass: A tall glass with foot and stem with a large, round deep bowl. As a unit of measure for serving size, 4 ounces is the most prevalent.

Wine Set: A decanter with matching wineglasses (may or may not include a matching tray).

Witch Ball: A spherical glass globe, usually 3 to 7 inches in diameter, and dating from early-eighteenth-century England. They were used to ward off evil, for fortune-telling, and in other superstitious ways.

Wrything Ornamentation: A decoration consisting of swirled ribbing or fluting.

BIBLIOGRAPHY

Angus-Butterworth. *British Table and Ornamental Glass*. New York: Arco Publishing Co., 1956.

Archer, Margaret and Douglas. *Imperial Glass*. Paducah, Ky: Collector Books, 1978.

Arwas, Victor. *Art Nouveau to Art Deco*. New York: Rizzoli International Publications Inc., 1977.

——. *Tiffany*. New York: Rizzoli International Publications, Inc. 1977.

Avila, George C. *The Pairpoint Glass Story*. New Bedford: Reynolds-Dewart Printing, Inc. 1968.

Baldwin, Gary, and Lee Carno. *Moser—Artistry in Glass 1857–1938*. Marietta, Ohio: Antique Publications, 1988.

Barber, Edwin A. *American Glassware*. Philadelphia: Press of Patterson & White Co., 1900.

Barbour, Harriot Buxton. *Sandwich: The Town That Glass Built*. Boston: Houghton Mifflin Co., 1948.

Barret, Richard Carter. *A Collector's Handbook of American Art Glass*. Manchester, Vt: Forward's Color Productions, 1971.

——. *A Collector's Handbook of Blown and Pressed American Glass*. Manchester, Vt: Forward's Color Productions, 1971.

——. *Popular American Ruby-Stained Pattern Glass*. Published by Richard Carter Barret and Frank L. Forward, 1968.

Battersby, Martin. *Art Nouveau: The Colour Library of Art*. Middlesex, England: The Hamlyn Publishing Group Ltd., 1969.

Batty, Bob H. *A Complete Guide to Pressed Glass*. Gretna, La: Pelican Publishing Co., 1978.

Belknap, E. McCamly. *Milk Glass*. New York: Crown Publishers, 1949.

Bennett, Harold and Judy. *The Cambridge Glass Book*. Iowa: Wallace-Homestead Book Co., 1970.

Bing, S. *Artistic America, Tiffany Glass and Art Nouveau*. Cambridge, Mass: Massachusetts Institute of Technology Press, 1970.

Bishop, Barbara & Martha Hassell. *Your Obdt. Servt., Deming Jarves*. Sandwich, Mass: The Sandwich Historical Society, 1984.

Blount, Berniece and Henry. *French Cameo Glass*. Des Moines, Iowa: published by authors, 1968.

Blum, John, et al. *The National Experience: A History of the United States*. New York: Harcourt Brace Jovanovich, 1981.

Boggess, Bill and Louise. *American Brilliant Cut Glass*. New York: Crown Publishers, 1977.

Bones, Frances. *The Book of Duncan Glass*. Des Moines, Iowa: Wallace-Homestead Book Co., 1973.

Bossaglia, Rossana. *Art Nouveau*. New York: Crescent Books, 1971.

Boston & Sandwich Glass Co. Boston: Lee Publications, 1968.

Bount, Henry and Berniece. *French Cameo Glass*. Des Moines, Iowa: Wallace-Homestead Book Co., 1968.

Bredehoft, Neila; George Fogg; and Francis Maloney. *Early Duncan Glassware: Geo. Duncan & Sons 1874–1892*. Boston: published by authors, 1987.

Bridgeman, Harriet, and Elizabeth Drury. *The Encyclopedia of Victoriana*. New York: Macmillan Co., 1975.

Brown, Clark W. *A Supplement to Salt Dishes*. Des Moines, Iowa: Wallace-Homestead Book Co., 1970.

The Cambridge Glass Co. Ohio: National Cambridge Collection, 1978.

Carved and Decorated European Glass. Rutland, Vt: Charles E. Tuttle Co., 1970.

Charleston, R. J. *English Glass*. London: George Allen and Unwin, 1984.

Charleston, Robert J. *Masterpieces of Glass: A World History from the Corning Museum of Glass*. New York: Harry N. Abrams, 1980.

Chase, Mark E., and Michael J. Kelly. *Contemporary Fast-Food and Drinking Glass Collectibles*. Radnor, Pa: Wallace-Homestead Book Co., 1988.

Cloak, Evelyn Campbell. *Glass Paperweights of the Bergstrom Art Center*. New York: Crown Publishers, 1969.

The Complete Book of McKee. Kansas City, Mo: The Tuga Press, 1974.

Contemporary Art Glass. New York: Crown Publishers, 1975.

Cosentino, Geraldine, and Regina Stewart. *Carnival Glass*. New York: Western Publishing Co., 1976.

Cousins, Mark. *20th Century Glass*. Secaucus, N.J.: Chartwell Books, 1989.

Cudd, Viola N. *Heisey Glassware*. Brenham, Tex.: Herrmann Print Shop, 1969.

Curtis, Jean-Louis. *Baccarat*. London: Thames and Hudson, 1992.

Daniel, Dorothy. *Cut and Engraved Glass 1771–1905*. New York: M. Barrows & Co., 1950.

———. *Price Guide to American Cut Glass*. New York: M. Barrows & Co., 1967.

Davis, Derek C. *English Bottles and Decanters 1650–1900.* New York: World Publications, 1972.

Davis, Derek C., and Keith Middlemas. *Colored Glass.* New York: Clarkson N. Potter, 1967.

Diamond, Freda. *The Story of Glass.* New York: Harcourt, Brace, and World, 1953.

Dibartolomeo, Robert E., ed. *American Glass, Volume II: Pressed and Cut.* New York: Weathervane Books, 1978.

Dorflinger C. & Sons. *Cut Glass Catalog 1881–1921.* Hanover, Pa: Everybody's Press, 1970.

Doros, Paul E. *The Tiffany Collection of the Chrysler Museum at Norfolk.* Norfolk, Va: Chrysler Museum, 1978.

Drepperd, Carl W. *ABC's of Old Glass.* Garden City, N.Y.: Doubleday & Company, 1968.

Duncan, Alastair. *Tiffany at Auction.* New York: Rizzoli International Publications, Inc. 1981.

Duncan, Alastair; Martin Eidelberg; and Neil Harris. *Masterworks of Louis Comfort Tiffany.* New York: Harry N. Abrams, 1989.

Ebbott, Rex. *British Glass of the 17th and 18th Centuries.* London: Oxford University Press, 1972.

Editors of the Pyne Press. *Pennsylvania Glassware 1870–1904.* Princeton: Pyne Press, 1972.

Edmonson, Barbara. *Old Advertising Spirits.* Oregon: Maverick Publications, 1988.

Edwards, Bill. *The Queen of Carnival Glass.* Paducah, Ky: Collector Books, 1976.

———. *The Standard Encyclopedia of Carnival Glass.* Paducah, Ky: Collector Books, 1982.

Ehrhardt, Alpha. *Cut Glass Price Guide.* Kansas City, Mo: Heart of America Press, 1973.

Elville, E. M. *English and Irish Cut Glass 1750–1950.* New York: Charles Scribner's Sons, 1951.

Ericson, Eric E. *A Guide to Colored Steuben.* 2 vols. Colorado: The Lithographic Press, 1963–1965.

Evers, Jo. *The Standard Cut Glass Value Guide.* Paducah, Ky: Collector Books, 1975.

Farrar, Estelle Sinclaire, and Jane Shadel Spillman. *The Complete Cut & Engraved Glass of Corning.* New York: Crown Publishers, 1978.

Fauster, Carl U. *Libbey Glass Since 1818.* Toledo, Ohio: Len Beach Press, 1979.

Florence, Gene. *The Collector's Encyclopedia of Akro Agate.* Paducah, Ky: Collector Books, 1975.

———. *The Collector's Encyclopedia of Depression Glass.* Paducah, Ky: Collector Books. 1990.

———. *Collectible Glassware from the 40's 50's 60's.* Paducah, Ky: Collector Books, 1992.

———. *Kitchen Glassware of the Depression Years.* Paducah, Ky: Collector Books, 1981.

Frantz, Susanne K. *Contemporary Glass: A World Survey From The Corning Museum of Glass.* New York: Henry N. Abrams, 1989.

Freeman, Larry. *Iridescent Glass.* Watkins Glen, N.Y.: Century House, 1964.

Gardner, Paul F. *Frederick Carder: Portrait of a Glassmaker.* Corning, NY: The Corning Museum of Glass, 1985.

———. *The Glass of Frederick Carder.* New York: Crown Publishers, 1971.

Grimmer, Elsa H. *Wave Crest Ware.* Des Moines, Iowa: Wallace-Homestead Book Co., 1979.

Grover, Ray and Lee. *Art Glass Nouveau.* Rutland, Vt: Charles E. Tuttle Co., 1967.

———. *Carved & Decorated European Art Glass.* Rutland, Vt: Charles E. Tuttle Co., 1967.

———. *English Cameo Glass.* New York: Crown Publishers, 1980.

Hand, Sherman. *The Collector's Encyclopedia of Carnival Glass.* Paducah, Ky: Collector Books, 1978.

Harrington, J. C. *Glassmaking at Jamestown: America's First Industry.* Richmond, Va: The Dietz Press, 1952.

Hartung, Marion. *Carnival Glass in Color.* Emporia, Kans.: published by author, 1967.

———. *Northwood Pattern Glass in Color.* Emporia, Kans.: published by author, 1969.

Haslam, Malcolm. *Marks and Monograms of the Modern Movement, 1875–1930.* New York: Charles Scribner's Sons, 1977.

Hastin, Bud. *Avon Collectibles Price Guide.* Kansas City, Mo: published by author, 1991.

Heacock, William. *The Encyclopedia of Victorian Colored Pattern Glass* (Books 1–4, 6–9). Marietta, Ohio: Antique Publications, 1974–1988.

———. *Fenton Glass: The First Twenty-five Years.* Marietta, Ohio: O-Val Advertising Corp. 1978.

———. *Fenton Glass: The Second Twenty-five Years.* Marietta, Ohio: O-Val Advertising Corp., 1980.

Heacock, William and Fred Bickenhauser. *The Encyclopedia of Victorian Colored Pattern Glass* (Book 5). Marietta, Ohio: Antique Publications, 1974–1988.

Heisey's Collector's Guide to Glassware for Your Table. Edited by Lyle Conder. Gas City, Ind: L-W Book Sales, 1984.

Hettes, Karel. "Venetian Trends in Bohemian Glassmaking in the 16th and 17th Centuries." *Journal of Glass Studies.* Volume 5. (1963).

Hollister, Paul, and Dwight Lanmon. *Paperweights.* Corning, NY: The Corning Museum of Glass, 1978.

Hollister, Paul, Jr. *The Encyclopedia of Glass Paperweights.* New York: Clarkson N. Potter, 1969.

Hotchkiss, John F. *Art Glass Handbook.* New York: Hawthorn Books, Inc. 1972.

————. *Carder's Steuben Glass Handbook and Price Guide*. New York: Hawthorn Books, 1972.

————. *Cut Glass Handbook and Price Guide*. Des Moines, Iowa: Wallace-Homestead Book Co., 1970.

House, Caurtman G. *Relative Values of Early American Patterned Glass*. Medina, N.Y.: published by author, 1944.

House of Collectibles. *The Official Price Guide to Carnival Glass*. New York: Random House, 1986.

————. *The Official Price Guide to Depression Glass*. New York: Random House, 1988.

Huether, Anne. *Glass and Man*. New York: J. B. Lippincott Co., 1965.

Hughes, G. Bernard. *English Glass for the Collector 1660–1860*. New York: Macmillan Co., 1968.

Hunter, Frederick William. *Stiegel Glass*. New York: Dover Publications, 1950.

Huxford, Sharon & Bob; eds. *Flea Market Trader*. Paducah, Ky: Collector Books, 1993.

Imperial Glass Corporation: *The Story of Handmade Glass*. Pamphlet published by Imperial (24 pp.), 1941.

Innes, Lowell. *Pittsburgh Glass 1797–1891: A History and Guide for Collectors*. Boston: Houghton Mifflin Co., 1976.

Jarves, Deming. *Reminiscences of Glassmaking*. Boston: Eastburn's Press, 1854.

Jefferson, Josephine. *Wheeling Glass*. Mount Vernon, Ohio: The Guide Publishing Co., 1947.

Jenks, Bill, and Jerry Luna. *Early American Pattern Glass 1850–1910*. Radnor, Pa: Wallace-Homestead Book Co., 1990.

Jokelson, Paul. *Sulphides: The Art of Cameo Incrustation*. New York: Thomas Nelson & Sons, 1968.

Ketchum, William C., Jr. *A Treasury of American Bottles*. New York: The Ridge Press, 1975.

Klamkin, Marian. *The Collector's Guide to Carnival Glass*. New York: Hawthorn Books, 1976.

————. *The Collector's Guide to Depression Glass*. New York: Hawthorn Books, 1973.

Klein, Dan, and Ward Lloyd. *The History of Glass*. New York: Crescent Books, 1989.

Koch, Robert. *Louis C. Tiffany, A Rebel in Glass*. New York: Crown Publishers, 1964.

Kovel, Ralph and Terry. *The Complete Antiques Price List*. New York: Crown Publishers, 1973, 1976, 1980, 1981, 1982, 1985, 1986, and 1990.

————. *The Kovel's Antique and Collectible Price List*. New York: Crown Publishers, 1992, 1993, 1994, and 1995.

————. *Kovels' Bottles Price List*. New York: Crown Publishers, 1992.

Krantz, Susan. *Contemporary Glass*. New York: Harry N. Abrams, 1989.

Krause, Gail. *Duncan Glass*. New York: Exposition Press, 1976.

Lafferty, James R. *The Forties Revisited*. Published by author, 1968.

Lee, Ruth Webb. *Early American Pressed Glass*. New York: Ferris Printing Co., 1946.

———. *Nineteenth Century Art Glass*. New York: M. Barrows and Co. 1952.

———. *Sandwich Glass*. New York: Ferris Printing Co. 1947.

Lindsey, Bessie M. *American Historical Glass*. Rutland, Vt. Charles E. Tuttle, 1967.

McClinton, Katharine Morrison. *Lalique for Collectors*. New York: Charles Scribner's Sons, 1975.

Mackay, James. *Glass Paperweights*. New York: Facts on File, 1973.

McKean, Hugh F. *The "Lost" Treasures of Louis Comfort Tiffany*. Garden City, N.Y.: Doubleday & Co., 1980.

McKearin, George and Helen. *American Glass*. New York: Crown Publishers, 1968.

———. *Nineteenth-Century Art Glass*. New York: Crown Publishers, 1966.

Madigan, Mary Jean. *Steuben Glass: An American Tradition in Crystal*. New York: Harry N. Abrams, 1982.

Manley, Cyril. *Decorative Victorian Glass*. New York: Von Nostrand Reinhold Co., 1981.

Mannoni, Edith. *Classic French Paperweights*. Santa Cruz, Calif.: Paperweight Press, 1984.

Mariacher, G. *Three Centuries of Venetian Glass*. (Translation.) Corning, NY: Corning Museum of Glass, 1957.

Markowski, Carol and Gene. *Tomart's Price Guide to Character & Promotional Glasses*. Radnor, Pa: Wallace-Homestead Book Co., 1990.

Marshall, Jo. *Glass Source Book*. London: Quarto Publishing Co., 1990.

Mebane, John. *Collecting Brides' Baskets and Other Glass Fancies*. Des Moines, Iowa: Wallace-Homestead Book Co., 1976.

Melvin, Jean S. *American Glass Paperweights and Their Makers*. New York: Thomas Nelson Publishers, 1970.

Miles, Dori, and Robert W. Miller, eds. *Wallace-Homestead Price Guide to Pattern Glass, 11th Edition*. Radnor, PA: Wallace-Homestead Book Co., 1986.

Miller, Robert. *Mary Gregory and Her Glass*. Iowa: Wallace-Homestead Book Co., 1972.

Miller, Robert, ed. *Wallace-Homestead Price Guide to Antiques and Pattern Glass*. Iowa: Wallace-Homestead Book Co., 1982.

Mish, C. Frederick, ed. in chief. *Webster's Ninth New Collegiate Dictionary*. Springfield, Mass: Merriam Webster Inc., Publishers. 1983.

Moore, N. Hudson. *Old Glass European and American*. New York: Tudor Publishing Co., 1924.

Neustadt, Egon. *The Lamps of Tiffany*. New York: The Fairfield Press, 1970.

Newark, Tim. *Emile Gallé.* London, England: Quintet Publishing Limited, 1989.

Newman, Harold. *An Illustrated Dictionary of Glass.* London: Thames and Hudson, 1977.

Nye, Mark. *Cambridge Stemware.* Miami: Mark A. Nye., 1985.

Oliver, Elizabeth. *American Antique Glass.* New York: Golden Press, 1977.

Padgett, Leonard E. *Pairpoint Glass.* Des Moines, Iowa: Wallace-Homestead Co., 1979.

Papert, Emma. *The Illustrated Guide to American Glass.* New York: Hawthorn Books, 1972.

Paul, Tessa. *The Art of Louis Comfort Tiffany.* New York: Exeter Books, 1987.

Pears, Thomas C., III. *Bakewell, Pears & Co. Glass Catalogue.* Pittsburgh: Davis & Warde, 1977.

Pearson, Michael and Dorothy. *American Cut Glass for the Discriminating Collector.* New York: Vantage Press, 1965.

———. *A Study of American Cut Glass Collections.* Miami: published by authors, 1969.

Pesatova, Zuzana. *Bohemian Engraved Glass.* Prague, Czechoslovakia: Knihtisk Publishing, 1968.

Peterson, Arthur G. *400 Trademarks on Glass.* Takoma Park, Md: Washington College Press, 1968.

Phillips, Phoebe; editor. *The Encyclopedia of Glass.* New York: Crown Publishers, 1981.

Pickvet, Mark. House of Collectibles. *The Official Price Guide to Glassware.* New York: Random House, 1995.

———. *Shot Glasses: An American Tradition.* Marietta, Ohio: Antique Publications, 1989.

Polak, Ada. *Glass, Its Tradition and Its Makers.* New York: G. P. Putnam's Sons, 1975.

Rainwater, Dorothy T. *Encyclopedia of American Silver Manufacturers.* New York: Crown Publishers, 1975.

Revi, Albert Christian. *American Art Nouveau Glass.* New York: Thomas Nelson and Sons, 1968.

———. *American Cut and Engraved Glass.* New York: Thomas Nelson and Sons, 1970.

———. *American Pressed Glass and Figure Bottles.* New York: Thomas Nelson and Sons, 1968.

———. *Nineteenth Century Glass.* New York: Galahad Books, 1967.

Ring, Carolyn. *For Bitters Only.* Boston: The Nimrod Press, 1980.

Rinker, Harry. *Warman's Americana and Collectibles.* Elkins Park, Pa: Warman Publishing Co., 1986.

Rose, James H. *The Story of American Pressed Glass of the Lacy Period 1825–1850.* Corning, NY: The Corning Museum of Glass, 1954.

Rossi, Sara. *A Collector's Guide To Paperweights.* Secaucus, N.J.: Wellfleet Books, 1990.

164646 14646666666646

Schmutzler, Robert. *Art Nouveau.* London: Thames & Hudson, 1978.

Schroeder, Bill. *Cut Glass.* Paducah, Ky: Collector Books, 1977.

Schroeder's Antiques Price Guide. Paducah, Ky: Collector Books, 1993.

Schroy, Ellen. *Warman's Glass.* Radnor, Pa: Wallace-Homestead Book Co., 1992.

Schwartz, Marvin D., ed. *American Glass Volume I: Blown and Molded.* New York: Weathervane Books, 1978.

Scott, Virginia R. *The Collector's Guide to Imperial Candlewick.* Athens, Ga: published by author, 1980.

Selman, Lawrence H. *The Art of the Paperweight.* Santa Cruz, Calif.: Paperweight Press, 1988.

Shuman John, III. *American Art Glass.* Paducah, Ky: Collector Books, 1988.

———. *Art Glass Sampler.* Des Moines, Iowa: Wallace-Homestead Book Co., 1978.

Shuman John, III, and Susan. *Lion Pattern Glass.* Boston: Branden Press, 1977.

Sichel, Franz. *Glass Drinking Vessels.* San Francisco: Lawton & Alfred Kennedy Printing, 1969.

Spillman, Jane Schadel. *American and European Pressed Glass in the Corning Museum of Glass.* Corning, NY: The Corning Museum of Glass, 1981.

———. *Glass From World's Fairs 1851–1904.* Corning, N.Y.: The Corning Museum of Glass, 1986.

———. *Glass, Tableware, Bowls, & Vases.* New York: Alfred A. Knopf, 1982.

Spillman, Jane Schadel and Susanne K. Frantz. *Masterpieces of American Glass.* Corning, N.Y.: The Corning Museum of Glass, 1990.

Stevens, Gerald. *Canadian Glass.* Toronto, Canada: The Ryerson Press, 1967.

———. *Early Canadian Glass.* Toronto, Canada: The Ryerson Press, 1967.

Stout, Sandra McPhee. *The Complete Book of McKee.* North Kansas City: Trojan Press, 1972.

Swan, Martha Louise. *American Cut and Engraved Glass of the Brilliant Period in Historical Perspective.* Illinois: Wallace-Homestead Book Co., 1986.

The Toledo Museum of Art. *Libbey Glass: A Tradition of 150 Years.* Toledo: The Toledo Museum of Art, 1968.

Toulouse, Julian. *Fruit Jars: A Collector's Manual.* Camden, N.J.: Thomas Nelson & Sons, 1969.

Traub, Jules S. *The Glass of Desire Christian.* Chicago: The Art Glass Exchange, 1978.

U.S. Patent Records.

Wakefield, Hugh. *19th Century British Glass*. New York: Thomas Yoseloff Publishing, 1961.

Warman, Edwin G. *American Cut Glass*. Uniontown, Pa: E. G. Warman Publishing, 1954.

Warren, Phelps. *Irish Glass*. New York: Charles Scribner's Sons, 1970.

Watkins, Lura Woodside. *Cambridge Glass*. Boston: Marshall Jones Co., 1930.

Weatherman, Hazel Marie. *Colored Glassware of the Depression Era*. Missouri: Weatherman Glass Books, 1974.

———. *Colored Glassware of the Depression Era II*. Missouri: Weatherman Glass Books, 1974.

———. *Fostoria: Its First Fifty Years*. Springfield, Ill.: The Weatherman's Publishers, 1979.

Weatherman, Hazel Marie, and Sue Weatherman. *The Decorated Tumbler*. Missouri: Glassbooks, 1978.

Webber, Norman W. *Collecting Glass*. New York: Arco Publishing Co., 1972.

Weiner, Herbert, and Freda Lipkowitz. *Rarities in American Cut Glass*. Houston, Tex: Collectors House of Books Publishing Co., 1975.

Whitehouse, David. *Glass of the Roman Empire*. Corning, N.Y.: The Corning Museum of Glass, 1988.

Whitmyer, Margaret and Kenn. *Children's Dishes*. Paducah, Ky: Collector Books, 1984.

Wilson, Jack D. *Phoenix & Consolidated Art Glass*. Marietta, Ohio: Antique Publications, 1989.

Wilson, Kenneth M. *New England Glass and Glassmaking*. New York: Thomas Y. Crowell Co., 1972.

Winter, Henry. *The Dynasty of Louis Comfort Tiffany*. Boston: Henry Winter, 1971.

Zerwick, Chloe. A Short History of Glass. New York: Harry N. Abrams , Publishers, 1990.

NUMEROUS ADVERTISEMENTS, TRADE CATALOGS, JOURNALS, AND OTHER PUBLICATIONS UTILIZED THAT ARE NOT LISTED ABOVE

American Glass Review

American Pottery and Glassware Reporter

Butler Brothers

Crockery and Glass Journal

The Crockery Journal

Enos' Manual of Old Pattern Glass

Journal of Glass Studies

The Pottery, Glass & Brass Salesman

COMPANY CATALOGS, BROCHURES, TRADE JOURNALS, AND ADVERTISEMENTS NOT INCLUDED ABOVE

Akro Agate Company
Anchor Hocking Glass Company
Baccarat Glass Company
Bakewell, Pears and Company
Bergen Cut Glass Company
Blenko Glass Company
Boston & Sandwich Glass Company
Boyd Art Glass Company
Bryce Brothers
Cambridge Glass Company
Central Glass Company
T. B. Clark & Company
Consolidated Lamp & Glass Company
C. Dorflinger & Sons
Duncan & Miller Glass Company
Durand Art Glass Company
Federal Glass Company
Fenton Art Glass Company
Fostoria Glass Company
H. C. Fry Glass Company
Gibson Glass Company
T. G. Hawkes & Company
Hazel Atlas Glass Company
A. H. Heisey & Company
J. Hoare & Company
Hobbs, Brocunier & Company
Hocking Glass Company
Imperial Glass Company

Indiana Glass Company
Jeannette Glass Company
King, Son, and Company
Lalique
Libbey Glass Company
McKee Brothers
Meriden Cut Glass Company
C. F. Monroe Company
Moser Glass Works
Mount Washington Glass Works
New England Glass Company
New Martinsville Glass Company
Northwood Glass Company
Paden City Glass Company
Pairpoint Manufacturing Company
Perthshire Paperweights Ltd.
Sabino Art Glass Company
H. P. Sinclaire Company
L. E. Smith Glass Company
Steuben Glass Works
Tiffany & Co.
Tipperary Crystal Company
Tuthill Cut Glass Company
Unger Brothers
U.S. Glass Company
Waterford Crystal Ltd.
Thomas Webb & Sons
Westmoreland Glass Company

AUCTION HOUSES, CATALOGS, BROCHURES, AND ADVERTISEMENTS

Sanford Alderfer Auction Company; Hatfield, Pennsylvania
Artfact, Inc.; Computer Auction Records' Services
James Bakker; Cambridge, Massachusetts
Ron Bourgeault & Company; Portsmouth, New Hampshire
Richard A. Bourne Company; Hyannis, Massachusetts
Bullock's Auction House; Flint, Michigan
Christie's and Christie's East; New York, New York
William Doyle Galleries; New York, New York
Dumouchelles; Detroit, Michigan
Early Auction Company; Milford, Ohio

Robert Eldred Company; East Dennis, Massachusetts
Garth's Auction, Inc.; Delaware, Ohio
Glass-Works Auctions; East Greenville, Pennsylvania
Guerney's; New York, New York
Leslie Hindman, Inc.; Chicago, Illinois
Milwaukee Auction Galleries; Milwaukee, Wisconsin
PK Liquidators; Flint, Michigan
David Rago; Trenton, New Jersey
Roan Brothers Auction Gallery; Cogan Station, Pennsylvania
SGCA Auctions; Flint, Michigan
Sotheby's; New York, New York

ANTIQUES SHOWS AND DEALERS

AA Ann Arbor Antiques Mall; Ann Arbor, Michigan
W. D. Adams Antique Mall; Howell, Michigan
Antique Gallery; Detroit, Michigan
The Antique Gallery; Flint, Michigan
The Antique Warehouse; Saginaw, Michigan
Ark Antiques; New Haven, Connecticut
Bankstreet Antiques Mall; Frankenmuth, Michigan
Bay City Antiques Center; Bay City, Michigan
Burton Gallery Antiques; Plymouth, Michigan
Cherry Street Antique Mall; Flint, Michigan
Flat River Antique Mall; Lowell, Michigan
Flushing Antique Emporium; Flushing, Michigan
Gallery of Antiques; Detroit, Michigan
Gilley's Antique Mall; Plainfield, Indiana
Hitching Post Antiques Mall; Tecumseh, Michigan
Indianapolis Antique Mall; Indianapolis, Indiana
Plymouth Antiques Mall; Plymouth, Michigan
Reminisce Antique Mall; Flint, Michigan
Showcase Antique Center; Sturbridge, Massachusetts
Water Tower Antiques Mall; Holly, Michigan

Special thanks to the numerous dealers and auction companies who allowed me to snap a few photographs and provided helpful advice on pricing and market trends.

INDEX